my **revision** notes

WJEC GCSE
HOSPITALITY & CATERING

Judy Gardiner

Orders: please contact Bookpoint Ltd, 130 Milton Park, Abingdon, Oxon OX14 4SB. Telephone: (44) 01235 827720. Fax: (44) 01235 400454. Lines are open from 9.00–5.00, Monday to Saturday, with a 24 hour message answering service. You can also order through our website www.hoddereducation.co.uk

If you have any comments to make about this, or any of our other titles, please send them to educationenquiries@hodder.co.uk

British Library Cataloguing in Publication Data

A catalogue record for this title is available from the British Library

ISBN: 9781444153897
First Edition Published 2011

Impression number   10 9 8 7 6 5 4
Year   2016 2015 2014 2013

Hachette UK's policy is to use papers that are natural, renewable and recyclable products and made from wood grown in sustainable forests.

The logging and manufacturing processes are expected to conform to the environmental regulations of the country of origin.

Cover photo from Reife Erdbeere auf weiß © Smileus/Fotolia

Typeset by Lee Churchill.

Printed in Spain for Hodder Education, an Hachette UK Company, 338 Euston Road, London, NW1 3BH.

Acknowledgements

The author would like to thank her husband for all his support, help and technical advice. She would also like to thank the many teachers attending INSET courses for their generous comments about previous books and their encouragement to write this revision guide.

The author and publishers would like to extend their thanks and gratitude to Jean Batchelor, Allison Candy, Susan Gould, Rhiannon Jones and Brigid O'Regan, whose contributions and attention to detail have been invaluable.

The author and publishers would like to thank the following for permission to reproduce material in this book:

p. 6 (left) © Smalik – Fotolia, (right) © Sally and Richard Greenhill/Alamy; p. 8 Photodisc/Getty Images; p. 13 (left and right) Sam Bailey/Hodder Education; p. 15 © Thomas Perkins/iStockphoto.com; p. 17 © Lucky Dragon USA – Fotolia; p. 18 © teracreonte – Fotolia; p. 22 © John Panella – Fotolia.com; p. 23 © Pål Espen Olsen/iStockphoto.com; p. 24 Sam Bailey/Hodder Education; p. 25 ©DWP – Fotolia; p. 26 © Mint Photography/Alamy; p. 28 (top) Crown copyright, (bottom) © Photodisc/Getty Images; p. 29 © Julián Rovagnati – Fotolia; p. 30 © Karen Struthers – Fotolia.com; p. 36 © Emrah Turudu/iStockphoto. com; p. 37 (left) © Marc Dietrich – Fotolia, (centre) © Ilya Zaytsev – Fotolia, (right) © Silkstock – Fotolia; p. 38 Sam Bailey/Hodder Education; p. 40 © thierryH – Fotolia; p. 41 © Steven May/Alamy; p. 52 © dutourdumonde – Fotolia; p. 67 © styleuneed – Fotolia

Crown copyright material is reproduced with the permission of the Controller of HMSO and the Queen's Printer for Scotland

Every effort has been made to obtain necessary permission with reference to copyright material. The publishers apologise if inadvertently any sources remain unacknowledged and will be glad to make the necessary arrangements at the earliest opportunity.

About the author

Judy Gardiner is Principal Examiner and a Consultative Moderator for GCSE Hospitality and Catering for a major awarding body. She is an education consultant with many years' experience teaching Hospitality and Catering courses. Now retired from full time teaching she spends her time training teachers, visiting schools, writing, moderating and examining.

How to **use** this **revision guide**

This revision guide is designed for use at the end of your course to provide key information, exam tips, personalised revision notes and quick tests to check progress.

It is set out topic by topic, in the same format as the textbook entitled *Hospitality and Catering for GCSE* Second Edition (ISBN 978 0 340 98682 0).

If you are studying:

- Hospitality and Catering Units 1 and 2 (Catering), you will need to study the first section of the book – Chapters 1 and 2
- Hospitality and Catering Units 3 and 4 (Hospitality), you will need to study the second section of the book – Chapters 3 and 4
- for the double award, you will need to study *all* chapters.

The revision guide is set out topic by topic, with the following features:

- Key facts – these are the essential facts that you need to learn
- Check your understanding – to check progress, knowledge and understanding
- Exam tips – ideas and suggestions for success in exams
- Revision activities – these provide a personal revision resource.

The revision guide can be used in several ways:

- to check that you have covered all the topics
- to track your progress:
  - there is a checklist at the front of the book to complete as you progress through the book
  - each chapter has tick boxes to complete as you progress through the topic
- to test your knowledge and understanding of each topic – there are questions for every topic (with an answer section at the end of the book)
- to give you ideas and tips for revision success
- to build your personal revision notes and flash cards using the 'Revision Activities'.

Many of the activities in the revision guide require you to make your own flash cards. This 'active revision' will help you remember the facts. The cards can be used individually, with friends or in larger groups to revise or test one another. The more practice you have recalling the facts, the more knowledgeable and confident you will become.

At the end of the book there are several examination questions, together with model answers and mark schemes. These give you the opportunity to see how other students have answered the questions and how marks have been awarded.

Good Luck!

Successful **revision**

Know your course
Read the topic checklist at the beginning of this book.

Make a revision timetable
Draw up a plan that covers all topics and set a realistic time for revision each week.

Revise effectively
What works best? 15–30 minutes of revision, followed by a break, usually works best. Start by revising favourite topics first to boost your confidence.

Make your revision active
Making brief notes, highlighting key points, drawing diagrams, using sticky notes, recording yourself, asking someone to test you and working with a friend are all good ways of revising.

Find the way of learning that suits you best
Not everyone learns in the same way – use key words, mnemonics, rhymes, pictures, diagrams, thought showers, colour coding, word association, etc. to trigger memory.

Study the style of questions used in the examination
Question papers contain a mix of short-answer questions, structured questions and a case study that is a series of questions about a particular topic.

Practise answering questions
Highlight or underline key words in the question, plan your response and ensure your answer is relevant.

Check your answers against the mark scheme
Ask your teacher for a copy of the mark scheme that was used to mark your mock examination. The mark scheme will highlight the quality of your responses against what the examiner was expecting.

Use old mark schemes for revising
A mark scheme is a great revision tool. You will not get the same questions again, but you will get to know the style of questions and the depth of response expected.

Prepare for examinations early
Do not try to cram lots of information at the last minute.

Allow time for final revision
Allow time for final revision to go over difficult or essential points, for example health, safety and hygiene, nutrition and menu planning.

Hospitality and Catering Examination Checklist

Use the following checklist to monitor your progress.

1&2 Hospitality and Catering Units 1 and 2 (Catering)

			Revised	Tested	Ready
6	1.1	The Catering Industry	☐	☐	☐
8	1.2	Food Service	☐	☐	☐
11	1.3	Job Roles, Employment and Training	☐	☐	☐
13	1.4	Health, Safety and Hygiene	☐	☐	☐
17	1.5	Legislation to include:			
17		Food Safety Act	☐	☐	☐
17		Food hygiene regulations	☐	☐	☐
17		HACCP (Hazard Analysis Critical Control Points)	☐	☐	☐
18		HASAWA – Health and Safety at Work Act 1974	☐	☐	☐
18		Risk assessment	☐	☐	☐
18		The Health and Safety Executive (HSE) five-point plan	☐	☐	☐
19		Fire regulations	☐	☐	☐
21	1.6	Food Preparation	☐	☐	☐
23	1.7	Cooking Methods	☐	☐	☐
24	1.8	Culinary Terms and Presenting Food	☐	☐	☐
27	1.9	Nutrition and Healthy Eating	☐	☐	☐
31	1.10	Menu Planning	☐	☐	☐
34	1.11	Portion Control and Costing	☐	☐	☐
36	1.12	Specialist Equipment	☐	☐	☐
38	1.13	Communication and Record-keeping	☐	☐	☐
40	1.14	Environmental Issues	☐	☐	☐
41	1.15	Food Packaging	☐	☐	☐
43	2.2	Catering Controlled Assessments	☐	☐	☐

3&4 Hospitality and Catering Units 3 and 4 (Hospitality)

			Revised	Tested	Ready

1.1 The Catering Industry

Key Facts

- Catering establishments provide food and/or drink.
- Catering establishments may be commercial (profit making) or non-commercial (non-profit making).
- Catering establishments may be residential (provide accommodation) or non-residential.
- Contract caterers provide food and drink for organisations such as businesses, schools and hospitals. Contract caterers are used to provide the food for functions such as garden parties, wedding receptions and dinner parties in private houses. Contract caterers may prepare and cook food in advance and deliver it to the venue, or they may cook it on site.

Café, commercial outlet

School cafeteria, non-commercial outlet

Check your understanding

1 Give three examples of commercial catering establishments.

2 Give three examples of non-commercial catering establishments.

3 Give three examples of residential catering establishments.

4 Give three examples of non-residential catering establishments.

5 Give four examples of organisations that would employ contract caterers.

6 Give three advantages of employing a contract caterer for a large garden party.

Exam tips

You should know about the role of a contract caterer and the advantages of employing a contract caterer to organise parties, functions and events.

Imagine someone else doing all the organising for a party you are holding – they would do all the planning, making and serving, leaving you free to enjoy the party with your guests. That's what a contract caterer does!

Revision Activity

Make a chart like the one below. The first two are examples to get you started.

Table 1.1.1

Outlet	Commercial or non-commercial	Residential or non-residential
McDonald's	commercial	non-residential
The Armed Forces	non-commercial	residential
Sea View Hotel	commercial	residential
School Meals	non commercial	non residential
HM Prison	non commercial	non residential
Suzy's Cafeteria	commercial	non residential
Bed and Breakfast	commercial	residential
Wine Bar	commercial	non residential
NHS Hospital	commercial	residential

1.2 Food Service

Revised

Key Facts

The range of food service systems includes:

- counter service
- table service
- transported meal systems
- cooking and/or serving of food from a trolley – Gueridon service.

Counter service is the most versatile of all systems and includes:

- cafeteria service (including multi-point service and free flow service) – customers queue at some type of counter, collect their food on a tray and pay for their food before they eat
- fast-food service – customers queue and pay for their food before they eat, e.g. McDonald's, Burger King, KFC, etc.
- vended service – customers use vending machines that dispense food and drink
- seated counter service – customers sit on stools round a bar where food and drink are served such as those found at railway stations, bars, etc.
- buffet service – may be assisted or self-service, customers help themselves to (or are served) food from a buffet table
- carvery service – customers queue to be served meat, then help themselves to vegetables and accompaniments.

Table service is used for a more personal service. With a waited service customers are served by waiters/waitresses (wait staff).

Transported meal systems include:

- airline food
- food on ferries, cruise ships, etc.
- food on trains
- hospital food

Fast-food outlet

Cooking and/or serving of food from a trolley involves using the Gueridon system, where food is flambéed, 'finished' or carved at the customer's table

Check your understanding

Tested

1 Why are vending machines likely to be found in railway stations?

2 Give three advantages of vended service.

3 Give three advantages of changing the serving of breakfast from waited service to buffet service in a hotel.

4 Why is fast food so popular?

5 Give three qualities needed by serving staff in a fast-food outlet.

6 Give three qualities needed by wait staff working in a five-star hotel.

7 Give three responsibilities of a restaurant manager.

Exam tips

Questions on food service are often linked to the **qualities** or **roles** of restaurant or kitchen staff.

You may also be asked to give the advantages of changing from one style of service to another, so make sure you know the basic service styles, their advantages and disadvantages and in which establishments they are likely to be used.

Below is a simple chart to show the advantages and disadvantages of different food service styles.

Table 1.2.1

Food service style	Advantages	Disadvantages
Counter service	<ul><li>Cost effective</li><li>Not many skills required</li><li>Food produced close to counter</li></ul>	<ul><li>Customers need to queue</li><li>Expensive equipment needed</li><li>Rates expensive as most outlets are in high street locations</li><li>Costly marketing and advertising</li></ul>
Plate service	<ul><li>Can control portion size and costs</li><li>Easy to serve</li><li>Low skill level required</li><li>Presentation of food consistent</li></ul>	<ul><li>Emphasis on chef's skills rather than service skills</li><li>Time consuming for chefs</li><li>Kitchen must be close to service area</li><li>Boring for serving staff</li></ul>
Family service	<ul><li>Less time consuming than silver service</li><li>Sociable so suits families</li><li>Customer can determine own portion size</li></ul>	<ul><li>Equipment and space required</li><li>Careful portion control from kitchen needed</li><li>Time consuming</li><li>Limits menu choice</li></ul>
Silver service	<ul><li>Customer has full and attentive service</li><li>Staff can promote further sales during service</li><li>Can cater for different clients and different functions</li></ul>	<ul><li>High labour costs (more staff needed)</li><li>Time consuming for staff</li><li>More service equipment required</li><li>Inexperienced staff may not serve professionally</li></ul>
Banquet service	<ul><li>Set menus can be used</li><li>Can serve many customers</li></ul>	<ul><li>High labour costs (a lot of staff needed)</li><li>A lot of equipment needed</li></ul>
Gueridon service	<ul><li>Opportunity for chefs to 'show off' and display skills</li><li>Relaxed dining experience for customers</li><li>Customer has personal attention</li></ul>	<ul><li>High labour costs (experienced chefs needed)</li><li>Menu costs high (found in à la carte restaurants)</li><li>Time consuming</li></ul>
Home delivery service	<ul><li>Convenient for customer</li><li>Emphasis on food production only</li><li>No food service space needed</li><li>No food service staff needed</li></ul>	<ul><li>Limited menu range can be offered</li><li>Presentation depends on packaging</li><li>Transport of food depends on local knowledge of staff</li><li>Prone to prank orders</li></ul>

Revision Activity

Table d'hôte cover
(place setting)

1 **Dinner (main course) knife and fork**

2 **Fish knife and fork**

3 **Soup spoon**

4 **Side plate and side knife (bread plate and butter knife)**

5 **Dessert (sweet) spoon and fork**

6 **Wine glass**

7 **Napkin (serviette)**

A la carte place
setting (cover)

1 **Fish knife and fork**

2 **Side plate and side knife**

3 **Base plate (show plate)**

4 **Napkin (serviette)**

5 **Wine glass**

- Study the diagram of the table d'hôte place setting shown.
- Study the diagram of the à la carte place setting shown.
- Practise table laying, so that you know the correct layout for table d'hôte and à la carte menus.
- Make a chart like the one below showing the main types of food service. The first one is an example to get you started. Note: There are other types of service you can add, e.g. silver service, family service.

Table 1.2.2

Types of service	Advantages	Disadvantages
Counter service	Customers pay before eating. Quick method of service.	Customers may need to queue.
Table service		
Carvery	*Self service.*	
Gueridon service		
Fast-food service		
Transported meal systems, e.g. airline food		

1.3 Job Roles, Employment and Training

Key Facts

Jobs in the catering industry are found in the following areas:

- **management** and **administration** – managers look after people, e.g. a restaurant manager 'manages' the restaurant brigade and reports directly to the manager. Administration staff, e.g. a storekeeper, often deal with paperwork
- **food preparation** – kitchen
- **food and drink service** – restaurant.

Jobs can be at the following levels:

- **management** – a manager or assistant manager or in large establishments; staff who are in charge of departments, e.g. an executive head chef or a restaurant manager
- **supervisory** – head chef, sous chef, restaurant manager, station head waiter
- **operative** – commis chef, kitchen porter, waiting staff.

Staff can be:

- **full time**
- **part time**
- **casual** or **seasonal**.

Training

There are employment opportunities at every level in the catering industry – from school leavers with no formal training to those with university degrees. Many establishments offer 'training on the job' or send employees on day-release/college courses.

Waitress

Check your understanding

1 Give five qualities needed by a waiter/waitress working in a seaside café.

2 Explain the role of a 'sous chef'.

3 Give three occasions when casual staff may be employed.

4 Give three differences between casual and part time staff.

Exam tips

This section relates to styles of food service, so revise the **two** topics **together**. Make sure you understand the different roles and responsibilities of a manager, a supervisor and an operative. Make sure you know the difference between full-time, part-time, casual and seasonal staff.

➤➤ Revision Activity

Complete two charts like those below showing the responsibilities
of different members of the kitchen and restaurant brigade.

Table 1.3.1

Job role (kitchen)	Operating level	Responsibilities
Head Chef	Management or supervisory (depending on size of establishment)	Training and supervision, health, safety and hygiene, menu planning, purchasing, costing and staff rotas
Sous Chef		
Commis Chef		

Table 1.3.2

Job role (restaurant)	Operating level	Responsibilities
Restaurant manager	Management or supervisory (depending on size of establishment)	Taking bookings, training and supervising staff, staff rotas, liaising with head chef, ensuring restaurant runs smoothly
Station head waiter		
Waiting staff		

1.4 Health, Safety and Hygiene

 Key Facts ————————————————————— Revised

Health, safety and hygiene underpin the catering syllabus. Learn the following topics really thoroughly and revise again just before the written examination.

Food poisoning

There are over 14,000 notified cases each year. The causes of food poisoning are:

- infected food handlers
- cross-contamination
- food prepared too far in advance
- not thawing frozen food properly
- use of pre-cooked food (bought ready-prepared, e.g. cook-chill)
- undercooking food (core temperature should be 75°C)
- not reheating food to a high enough temperature (minimum 72°C)
- hot-holding food below 63°C
- cooling too slowly through danger zone
- use of leftovers, e.g. **cooked rice** is a high-risk food, but is often used again for salads, stir fries, etc.

Shellfish

Cooked rice

> **Remember these sayings.**
>
> Bugs can't be seen
> – so give it a clean!
>
> Heat right to eat right!
>
> If in doubt, throw it out!
>
> Cooked above raw
> – that's the law!

Food poisoning is caused by harmful (**pathogenic**) bacteria. Types of food poisoning include **E. Coli** (raw and undercooked meats), **Salmonella** (chicken and eggs), **Listeria** (soft cheeses and pate), **Staphylococcus** (nose and throat of humans). Salmonella causes more than 80 per cent of food poisoning cases in the UK.

High-risk foods are usually moist and high in protein, e.g. cooked poultry, cooked meats, dairy produce, cooked rice, soups, sauces and stocks, shellfish, raw eggs in mayonnaises.

Low-risk foods are usually low in moisture, low in protein, high in fat, e.g. lard, butter and hard cheese, acidic, or high in salt, e.g. dried (dehydrated) foods, pickled foods, jams and other preserves, bacon, and chemically preserved foods.

The **symptoms of food poisoning** are abdominal pains, nausea, sickness, diarrhoea, fever.

The 'three Cs'

Remember the 'three Cs' – keep food **cold**, **clean** and **covered**. Bacteria need food, warmth, moisture and time to multiply.

Key temperatures

Table 1.4.1

−18°C	Freezer temperature (bacteria are dormant – not dead at low temperatures)
1°C–5°C	Fridge temperature (never put <u>hot</u> food into a fridge – it raises temperature to an unsafe level)
5°C–63°C	The **danger zone** – bacteria multiply rapidly, especially at room or body temperature
63°C +	Hot-holding of food
72°C	Two minutes (minimum core temp of reheated food)
75°C	Core temperature of cooked food
100°C	Boiling water – most germs killed
170°–190°C	Temperature of hot oil in a deep fat fryer (extreme care is needed when frying)

Food hygiene regulations

These regulations are to prevent outbreaks of food poisoning. There are three main areas:

1   Food premises – these must be clean and well maintained, with hot and cold water available, good toilet facilities, clothing lockers, first aid, fire prevention, equipment in good condition, adequate storage facilities, good ventilation.

2   Personal hygiene – correct footwear, correct uniform, headwear, good personal habits, good health and high standard of personal cleanliness.

3   Hygienic practices – food stored correctly, waste disposed of hygienically, good cleaning schedules, no animals in food areas, etc.

Accident prevention

Think about *all* aspects of working in a catering kitchen and say how you could prevent accidents from occurring:

- **floor** – grease free, spillages mopped up, wet floor notices
- **light equipment**, e.g. knives – care when using
- **heavy equipment** – care when lifting, moving
- **electrical equipment** – turn off after use, no water nearby
- **clothing** – worn for protection, what? why?
- **workers** – no running in kitchen, organised, sensible
- **storage areas** – equipment and food easily accessible
- **fire prevention** and **fire procedures**
- **cleaning** – clean kitchens are less likely to cause accidents, especially falls
- **care when using hot ovens** and **fryers**, etc. to avoid burns/scalds.

Important personal hygiene rules

Wash hands before handling food	**Do not cough or sneeze over food**
Keep nails short and clean	**Cover cuts with blue waterproof plasters**
Do not wear jewellery	**Never lick fingers**
Wear clean whites	**Taste food with a clean metal spoon**

Accident procedures

All accidents must be reported, even if an injury does not appear serious at first. Records must include:

- name (of injured person)
- sex (of injured person)
- exact time and date (of accident)
- place (where accident occurred)
- what happened
- what part of the body was injured and how badly
- whether first aid was given
- further treatment (e.g. sent to doctor or hospital)
- supervisor
- witnesses
- whether worker was doing his job at the time of the accident.

Mop and bucket

First aid

By law there has to be at least one first-aid box and one named first aider for every 150 people. You need to know about the treatment for the following:

- **Cuts** – wash, dry and apply a blue, waterproof plaster. If bleeding does not stop, apply pressure.
- **Burns and scalds** – a burn is caused by dry heat, e.g. a hot pan. A scald is caused by moist heat, e.g. steam or boiling liquids. Run under cold water for at least 10 minutes or until the stinging sensation stops. Do not apply creams. Do not 'pop' blisters. If burn is larger than a 10p piece seek medical help.
- **Fat burns** are always serious because of the cooking temperature of the fat. Seek medical help immediately.
- **Falls** – if serious, do not move patient but seek medical help. For less serious falls, allow patient to move to a sitting, then standing position slowly. If patient feels faint put their head between their knees. Check for other injuries.

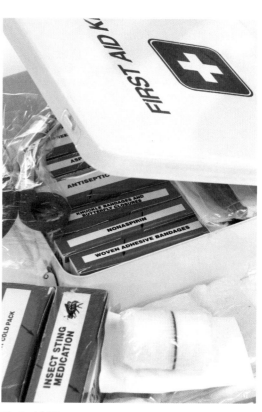

First-aid kit

Check your understanding
Tested

1 Name two food poisoning bacteria.

2 Give three symptoms of food poisoning.

3 Why do chefs wear a hat?

4 Give three personal hygiene rules.

5 Give three food hygiene rules.

6 Give three kitchen hygiene rules.

7 Give the first-aid treatment for a burn.

8 Why are blue plasters used in catering?

9 What is the temperature of: **i.** a fridge; **ii.** a freezer; **iii.** hot-held food?

> **Exam tip**
>
> Do not confuse personal hygiene with food hygiene!

Exam tips

Knowledge of 'key temperatures' is particularly important as many of the extended questions at the end of the examination paper require knowledge of health, safety and hygiene.

Remember to use your knowledge of key temperatures in the 'essay style' questions at the end of the written paper. For example, if answering a question on serving food for a cold buffet, include the storage of food in a refrigerator beforehand at a temperature of 5°C, keeping food out of the danger zone (5°C–63°C) and the four-hour rule for displaying cold food.

Revision Activity

Completed ☐

Prepare some small flash cards with temperatures on one side and what they represent on the other. Two examples are given here to start you off. Revise key temperatures regularly so they become second nature.

63°C

Hot-holding temperature

−18°C

Freezer temperature

1.5 Legislation

Health, safety and hygiene underpin the catering specification. You must know about the following Acts and legislation.

Food Safety Act

This covers:

1 Food quality.
2 Food safety.
3 Food composition.
4 Food labelling and advertising.

Under the Act, **Environmental Health Officers** (EHOs):

- can close dirty premises immediately
- can impose fines of £20,000 or six months' imprisonment
- can take legal action for manslaughter.

All premises must be registered with the local authority and can be inspected **at any time** by an EHO. The Food Safety Act links closely with Hygiene Regulations and HACCP.

Environmental Health Officer

Food hygiene regulations

These regulations are to prevent outbreaks of food poisoning.

There are three main areas:

1 **Food premises** – these must be clean and well maintained, have hot and cold water available, good toilet facilities, clothing lockers, first aid, fire prevention, equipment in good condition, adequate storage facilities and good ventilation.
2 **Personal hygiene** – correct footwear, uniform, headwear, good personal habits, good health and cleanliness.
3 **Hygienic practices** – food stored correctly, waste disposed of hygienically, good cleaning schedules, no animals in food areas, etc.

HACCP (Hazard Analysis Critical Control Points)

Think of the flow of work through a catering kitchen. Make sure you think of at least three points to write about each danger/hazard and how to prevent the danger/hazard from occurring. The areas to consider are:

- purchase of food – buy from reputable suppliers
- receipt of food – checking deliveries – for temperature, quality points
- storage of food – remember **dry**, **chilled** and **frozen**
- preparation of food to avoid cross contamination – how?
- cooking of food – cook thoroughly (above 75ºC)
- cooling – cool through the danger zone as quickly as possible (5ºC–63ºC)
- hot-holding – above 63ºC
- reheating – *not* for high-risk groups (above 72ºC for two minutes)
- chilled storage – between 1ºC and 5ºC
- serving – obey the four-hour rule for cold food and the two-hour rule for hot food.

HASAWA (Health and Safety at Work Act 1974)

This covers *all* aspects of **health and safety** of employees.

- Employers must provide <u>safe</u> working areas (includes use of machinery and tools, adequate working space, good temperature control (i.e. ventilation and heating), supervision, instruction and training of staff, cleaning, first aid, clothing, etc.
- Employees must also take care of their own health and safety, not endanger others and not misuse premises or equipment.

Green information signs

Risk assessment

A risk assessment is a summary of what (in your place of work) could cause harm to people. A risk assessment is carried out in the following way:

- Identify risks or hazards, e.g. fire risk, back problems from lifting heavy loads, etc.
- Decide who may be harmed and how.
- Evaluate risks and decide on the precautions that need to be taken.
- Implement (put into practice) precautions.
- Review risk assessment regularly and update when necessary.

The Health and Safety Executive (HSE) five-point plan

Health and safety law states that organisations must:

- provide a written health and safety policy (if they employ five or more people)
- assess risks to employees, customers, partners and any other people who could be affected by their activities
- arrange for the effective planning, organisation, control, monitoring and review of preventive and protective measures
- ensure they have access to competent health and safety advice
- consult employees about their risks at work and current preventive and protective measures.

Failure to meet these requirements could have serious consequences. Sanctions and punishments include fines and imprisonment.

Fire regulations

Fire prevention

- Fire alarms should be tested weekly.
- Staff should be instructed in the use of fire-fighting equipment.

Fire procedures

- Raise the alarm.
- Call the fire brigade.
- If possible, turn off gas supply, electricity and fans.
- Try to fight the fire with the appropriate extinguisher or fire blanket but *do not put yourself in danger*.
- Close doors and windows.
- Leave the building and go to the assembly point.
- *Do not* delay raising the alarm or calling the fire brigade.
- *Do not* use lifts.
- *Do not* stop to collect your belongings.
- Care must be taken to use the correct fire extinguisher.
- Although it may be possible to extinguish a small fire, *never* put yourself or others in danger.

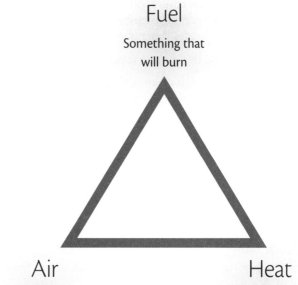

Fuel
Something that will burn

Air
Oxygen in the air will keep the fire going

Heat
E.g. electrical equipment, a gas ring that has been left on

Check your understanding
Tested ☐

1 What powers does an EHO have under the Food Safety Act?

2 What is the main aim of the HASAWA?

3 What do the letters HACCP stand for?

4 What is risk assessment?

5 Give three rules to follow in the event of a fire in a hotel kitchen.

6 What do the following signs indicate?

Revision Activity ———————————————————— Completed ☐

Prepare a set of flash cards. One good way to do this activity is to buy a set of blank postcards. Write the name of the Act on the front of the card and the main points of the law (as set out in the Act) on the back. Learn thoroughly!

Here is an example to help you start.

Hygiene regulations

Personal hygiene – correct uniform, correct footwear, correct headwear, good personal habits, cleanliness, good health

Hygienic practices – food and equipment stored correctly, good cleaning schedules, waste disposed of correctly, no animals or pests in food areas

Food premises – clean and well maintained, hot and cold water available, good toilet facilities and lockers for staff, first aid, fire prevention, equipment in good order, adequate storage facilities, good lighting and ventilation

1.6 Food Preparation

Key Facts — Revised

Cookery skills include:

- cake making – rubbing-in method, creaming method, whisking method, melting method and the one-stage or all-in-one method (that replaces creaming)
- bread making
- biscuit, scone and muffin making
- pastry making – types (shortcrust, sweet pastry, choux pastry, puff pastry, etc.) and knowing the method of making at least one of them
- sauce making – blended and roux sauces.

The **basic commodities** used in catering include:

- meat and poultry
- fish
- eggs
- dairy products
- rice, pasta and other cereals
- fruit and vegetables
- convenience products.

Check your understanding — Tested

1   List four methods of cake making and a cake made by each method.

2   A batch of scones turns out like biscuits. What could have gone wrong?

3   Give three rules to follow when making shortcrust pastry.

4   Give three reasons why convenience foods are popular with caterers.

5   Rice and pasta dishes are often quite bland. Discuss ways in which rice and pasta can be made more appealing.

Exam tips

Remember to use your own experience of **food preparation** when answering questions on this topic. For example, if answering a question on chicken, try to think of the chicken dishes you have made in your practical sessions and include them in your answer.

When answering a question on commodities you should think about the following:
- the types available
- uses and versatility (can it be used in sweet and savoury dishes, served hot and/or cold, raw and/or cooked)
- ease of preparation and cooking
- cost
- storage
- colour, flavour and texture
- nutritive value.

Write notes about different commodities. Start with these examples: eggs, cheese, chicken, potatoes, rice, pasta, fresh fruit. Then add other commodities that you have used during the course to your list, e.g. milk, meat.

One good way to do this activity is to make a series of cards (or buy a set of blank postcards). On one side put a picture of the commodity and on the other side write about the commodity.

Here is an example to help you start.

It will not matter if you miss out one or two points, as long as you give specific examples in the points you do remember. When you have completed a few cards it will become easier.

Types – whole, breast, legs, thighs, wings, etc.

Uses – roast dinner, casseroles, stuffed, vol au vents, fajitas, kebabs, fried, grilled, served in sauces, served cold in sandwiches, wraps and for buffets

Prep – chicken should be defrosted thoroughly (if frozen) and prepared close to cooking/serving time

Cooking – should be cooked thoroughly (core temperature 75°C) to avoid salmonella food poisoning

Cost – chicken is economical to buy

Storage – chicken is a high-risk food and must be stored in a refrigerator below 5°C

Colour, flavour and texture – chicken is quite bland. Flavour and colour can be added with stuffing, herbs, spices, marinades and sauces

Nutritive value – HBV protein, Vitamin B, low in fat

1.7 Cooking Methods

Key Facts

We cook food to:
- make it easier to digest
- add flavour
- make it look more appetising
- make it smell more appealing
- make it safer to eat
- prevent spoilage
- increase keeping qualities.

The **main methods** of cooking are:
- **cooking in water** – boiling, simmering, poaching, steaming, pressure cooking, stewing and blanching
- **cooking in fat** – dry frying, shallow frying, stir-frying, deep-fat frying, braising, flambéing and fondue cookery
- **cooking in an oven** – baking, roasting, casseroling, grilling and microwaving.

Check your understanding

1 Give four safety rules to follow when deep-fat frying.

2 Give two reasons for the popularity of each of the following cooking methods: grilling, stir-frying, barbecuing, deep-fat frying, microwaving.

3 Suggest three cuts of beef suitable for grilling.

4 Suggest how delicate food can be protected when deep-fat frying.

Exam tips

Questions on cooking methods are likely to focus on:
- the **popularity** of certain methods, e.g. stir-frying, barbecuing
- important **safety points**, especially for frying, grilling and microwaving
- **types of food/dishes** that can be cooked by each method and any special preparation of the food that is needed before cooking.

Note: If the question is linked to nutrition or healthy eating you need to know how nutrients are likely to be affected by the choice of cooking method. For example:
- Water-soluble vitamins (Vitamins B and C) dissolve in water.
- Protein 'sets' or 'coagulates' at quite low temperatures.
- Stir-frying is considered a healthy method of cooking because the cooking time is short and so most nutrients are retained.

Revision Activity

Develop a set of your own flash cards indicating methods of cooking. Use the examples given under the heading 'main methods' shown above, e.g. frying, boiling, etc. Put a picture of the method on one side and important points to remember on the other.

Here is an example to help you start.

Stir-frying

Why popular?
Quick, colourful, good textured food, healthy option

Why healthy?
Because little fat is used, quick cooking retains nutrients

Foods that can be stir-fried include good-quality meat, e.g. steak, chicken, pork, and vegetables such as sweetcorn, carrots, onions, mushrooms, peppers, mange tout, beansprouts, etc.

1.8 Culinary Terms and Presenting Food

Key Facts

Learn the following terms and their meanings. There will be a question on these on every examination paper!

Table 1.8.1

Terms used	Meaning
accompaniments	Items offered separately to main dish, e.g. vegetables and sauces
al dente	Literally means 'to the tooth', i.e. firm to the bite
au gratin	Sprinkled with cheese and/or breadcrumbs and browned under a grill
bain-marie	A container of water used to keep foods hot without fear of burning or to cook delicate foods
brûlée	'Burned', e.g. crème brûlée or burned cream
bouquet garni	A bundle of herbs
coulis	A sauce made of fruit or vegetable purée
croutons	Cubes of toasted or fried bread
en croûte	'In a pastry case', e.g. salmon en croûte
entrée	A meat dish usually served as a main course
flambé	To cook with flame by 'burning' away alcohol, e.g. crêpes suzette
garnish	A savoury decoration for food, trimmings served with a main item
julienne	Thin, matchstick-sized strips of vegetables
marinade	A richly spiced liquid used to give flavour to and help tenderise meat and fish
mise-en-place	'Put in place', i.e. preparation either before starting to cook or before serving
purée	A smooth mixture made from food passed through a sieve or liquidised in a food processor
reduce	To concentrate a liquid by boiling or simmering
roux	A mixture of fat and flour used as a basis for a sauce
sauté	To toss in hot fat, e.g. sauté potatoes

Presenting food

Learn the following rules for presenting food:

- Dishes must have a range of colour, texture, flavour and shape.
- Dishes (and food) should be hot or cold as necessary.
- Dishes should be the correct consistency.
- Use stylish plates (dramatic shapes or colours) to frame the food.
- Food should not be crowded on the plate.
- Food needs to be 'natural' in colour whenever possible.

A beautifully presented plate of food

- Food should be garnished or decorated appropriately.
- Rich foods should be served in small portions.
- Sauces and relishes etc. should be served separately.
- Food should have a pleasing smell/aroma to tempt appetite.
- Plates should be spotlessly clean.
- Food should be kept off the rim.

Food has to be presented well in order to appeal to customers. It is important to maintain a high standard of presentation throughout service time, particularly for buffets and carvery service.

The most important points to consider when presenting food attractively are:

- **colour** – of the food itself and the plates/dishes used for serving food
- **flavour** – food should be well seasoned
- **texture** – food should have a variety of textures including crunchy, soft, chewy and crisp
- **shape** – different shapes add interest to food. This could be shape of the food itself, e.g. curly lettuce leaves, or shapes created when food is stacked attractively
- **temperature** – food should be hot or cold as necessary and served out of the danger zone (5°C to 63°C)
- **time** – food should be served quickly so that it does not cool down (or heat up) unnecessarily
- **customers' needs** (including specific dietary needs)
- **cooking** and presentation skills
- **environment**, i.e. creating a good 'meal experience' for customers.

Presenting food for a buffet:

- Large serving dishes need to remain attractive throughout service.
- Add height – the use of raised platforms to display food.
- Simplicity – it is important to make the food look attractive. Over-decoration will detract from the food.
- Careful use of garnish and decoration to add colour, e.g. dressed salmon with cucumber and lemon.
- Good use of fruit and vegetables to enhance appearance of food.
- Use of flags or labels on foods, which is especially important for vegetarians.
- Introduce a variety of shapes with serving dishes as well as food to add interest.
- For self-serve buffets, include tongs and serving spoons for every dish.
- Good portion control, e.g. cutting lines, garnish or decoration on foods like gateaux and cheesecakes.
- Hot foods (if served) should be at the end of the buffet service so that they do not cool while customers select cold food.
- Constant cleaning down by wait staff to ensure buffet looks good throughout service.

A well-presented buffet

Presenting food for carvery service:

- Food is on display, therefore needs to look appetising throughout service to reflect high standards of hygiene and safety.

- Customers may arrive at any time during service – the food needs to be hot, attractive and well presented, whether they arrive early or late.

- Fresh dishes of food should be brought out as soon as dishes get low.

- Remember dishes that are prepared first should be served first: first in, first out.

- If lids are used to keep food hot, lift carefully to avoid condensation falling onto food or serving table.

- Give clean serving spoons with replacement dishes of food.

A chef carving at a carvery

- Older food should not be added to the replacement food in view of the customers.

- Carvery table should be constantly checked and cleaned (to replenish nearly empty dishes, wipe up spills, etc.).

- Carving knives and forks need to be cleaned after each service.

- Different carving knives could be used for each type of meat if wipes are not available.

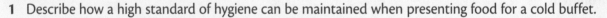

Check your understanding

Tested

1 Describe how a high standard of hygiene can be maintained when presenting food for a cold buffet.

2 Explain the importance of colour when presenting food.

3 Explain the importance of portion control when presenting food for a buffet.

Exam tips

Questions on food presentation can relate to **types of menu** or **hygiene and safety** factors. Think about your practical sessions when answering questions on food presentation, and about the 'look' of food that tempts you to eat.

- Does the size of the dish make a difference (an overcrowded plate or too large a plate for the size of the portion)?
- Does the colour of the dish (or the food) make a difference?
- Does the cleanliness of the dish make a difference?
- Does a garnish or decoration make a difference?
- Does the temperature of the food make a difference?
- Does the texture of the food make a difference?
- Does the shape and overall appearance of the food on the plate make a difference?
- Does the smell (aroma) of the dish make a difference?

Revision Activity

Completed

Try serving food on different colour backgrounds (a cheap way to do this is by using paper napkins). Notice how some colours make food more attractive while other colours clash with food or make it look unattractive.

Remember to use this knowledge in your examination.

1.9 Nutrition and Healthy Eating

 **Key Facts** ———————————————— Revised ☐

The **main nutrients** and their functions in the body are:

- **protein** – the 'body-builder' – needed for growth and repair of body cells
- **carbohydrates** – provide energy
- **fats** – provide energy and body warmth
- **vitamins** – give protection against disease
- **minerals** – give protection against disease.

The following are not nutrients but have important functions in the body:

- **fibre** and NSP (non-starch polysaccharides) – to rid the body of waste and prevent constipation
- **water** – to maintain body temperature, help digestion, lubricate joints and help remove waste from the body.

More about the main nutrients

Protein

Protein is **the most important nutrient** because it is the only one that can be used for growth and repair of body cells – no other nutrient can do this!

There are two types:

- **high biological value** – those that contain the essential amino acids from which the body can manufacture the rest (mostly animal proteins with the exception of soya)
- **low biological value** – those that do not contain the essential amino acids (mostly vegetable proteins).

Proteins that are suitable for vegetarians include textured vegetable protein (TVP), tofu, (soya bean curd) and Quorn.

Carbohydrates

Carbohydrates provide the body with energy. Carbohydrate foods can be starchy or sugary. Starchy foods, e.g. rice, pasta, potatoes, bread and cereals, provide the body with other nutrients and give long-lasting energy. Sugary foods, e.g. sugar, jam, marmalade and sweets, often provide no other nutrients and can cause tooth decay. Eating too many carbohydrates can lead to obesity.

Fats

Fats provide the body with energy and because they form an insulating layer under the skin they also provide body warmth. Saturated fats (mostly animal fats like butter and lard) are more harmful than unsaturated or polyunsaturated fats (found in some margarines and olive oil).

Eating too much fat can cause obesity, high cholesterol, coronary heart disease, halitosis (bad breath) and Type 2 diabetes.

Vitamins

Vitamins are needed in only tiny amounts. The main vitamins and their uses are:

- Vitamin A – prevents night blindness
- Vitamin B group – essential for the nervous system, help release energy from carbohydrate foods
- Vitamin C – supports the immune system, helps body absorb iron, forms connective tissue
- Vitamin D – known also as the 'sunshine vitamin', works with calcium to maintain strong bones and teeth.

Minerals

Minerals are also needed in only tiny amounts. The main minerals are calcium and iron:

- Calcium is needed for strong bones and teeth.
- Iron is needed for the formation of red blood cells. A lack of iron can cause anaemia.

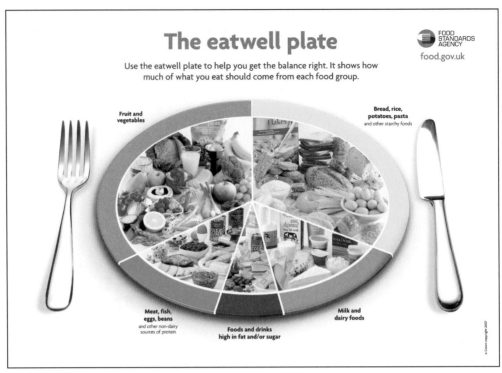

The eatwell plate

Use the eatwell plate to help you get the balance right. It shows how much of what you eat should come from each food group.

FOOD STANDARDS AGENCY
food.gov.uk

Fruit and vegetables

Bread, rice, potatoes, pasta and other starchy foods

Meat, fish, eggs, beans and other non-dairy sources of protein

Foods and drinks high in fat and/or sugar

Milk and dairy foods

The eatwell plate

Healthy eating

The key ways to eat healthily are:

- Eat less fat (and have a healthier heart).
- Eat less sugar (to prevent tooth decay and obesity).
- Eat less salt (to prevent high blood pressure).
- Eat more fibre (to maintain a healthy digestive system).
- Eat five a day of fruit and vegetables (rich in fibre, vitamins and minerals).
- Avoid alcohol. Drink plenty of water.

Special diets

Vegetarian diets

There are two main types of vegetarian:

- lacto-vegetarians, who eat no animal (meat, poultry or fish) flesh but do eat animal products, i.e. dairy foods
- vegans, who eat no animal products of any kind.

Religious diets

Different religions have different dietary restrictions. For example:

- Muslims do not eat pork. They eat halal meat (i.e. from an animal that has been slaughtered in a special way according to the religious law).
- Hindus do not eat beef.
- Some Sikhs do not eat meat or fish.
- Jews do not eat pork, bacon, ham, shellfish or eels. They do not eat milk and meat at the same time. They eat kosher meat (i.e. that has been prepared in accordance with Jewish dietary guidelines).

Medical diets

There are many medical reasons why people cannot eat certain foods, including:

- diseases such as diabetes
- allergies such as nut allergy
- food intolerances such as gluten or lactose intolerance.

  WARNING
This product may contain nuts

Sugar-free chocolates for people with diabetes

Check your understanding

1 Name two nutrients found in cheese.

2 Explain why the body needs fibre.

3 Why should iron-rich foods be eaten with foods rich in Vitamin C?

4 Name the two nutrients that are needed for healthy teeth and bones.

5 Match up the two halves of the following statements correctly.

A vegan	should avoid sugary foods.
A lactose intolerant person	lacks iron.
A person with anaemia	does not eat animal flesh or animal products.
A diabetic	does not eat milk or milk products.

> **Exam tip**
>
> There is a lot of information to learn about nutrition, but if you have revised this topic well it could make a difference to your final grade.

What nutrients are used for

Nutrients have one of three uses:

- body building (protein)
- providing energy (carbohydrates and fats)
- protecting the body from illness and disease (vitamins and minerals).

> **Exam tip**
>
> All food contains nutrients but no food is 'full of' a specific nutrient – do not use this phrase when answering an examination question.

The foods you tend to eat most of will provide you with the energy needed to get you through the day (usually starchy foods like cereals, bread, pasta, potatoes and rice). If asked a question about vitamins or minerals, think about the size of a vitamin or mineral tablet – one small tablet could not possibly provide you with the energy needed to get through the day!

The word **vitamin** comes from the word **vital**, in this case vital for good health.

Minerals are needed in **minute** quantities. Both words start with '**min**' to help you remember.

▶ Revision Activity 1

Make a series of work cards. On one side of the card draw or place a picture of the main food groups and on the other list their uses (functions in the body) and where they are found (sources of the nutrient). Two examples are shown here.

Vitamins and minerals – protect the body from illness and disease

Main sources are fruit and vegetables

Vitamin A (visual purple) carrots, tomatoes

Vitamin B (nervous system) cereals, meat, fish

Vitamin C (immune system) citrus fruit, kiwi fruit

Vitamin D (bones and teeth) cheese, butter, marg

Iron (red blood cells) red meat, cocoa, eggs

Calcium (bones and teeth) milk, cheese, green veg

Carbohydrates – provide the body with energy

Main sources are bread, pasta, potatoes, breakfast cereals and rice

Types of carbohydrate are:

- **starch** – energy from these foods is released slowly so make us feel full longer
- **sugars** – these provide instant energy
- **NSP (non-starch polysaccharides)** – complex carbohydrates which are not absorbed by the body.

Revision Activity 2

Completed ☐

- Draw round your hands on a piece of A4 paper.
- Put heading at the top: 'How does eating "five a day" relate to healthy eating?'
- Fill in the fingers of the left hand with five of the healthy eating guidelines and see how fruit and vegetables 'fit into' the guidelines.

Healthy eating

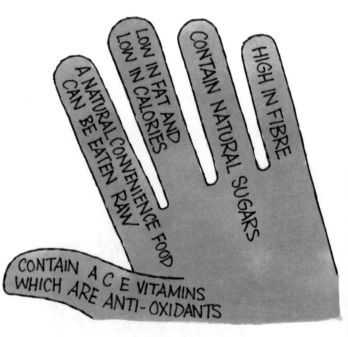

'Five a day' fruit and veg

1.10 Menu Planning

Key Facts — Revised

Before starting to plan a menu, consider the 'four Ws':

- **Who** is going to eat the food (age, sex, occupation, specific dietary needs)?
- **When** is it going to be eaten (time of year, time of day)?
- **Where** is it going to be served/eaten (venue, space and facilities available)?
- **What** type of food is going to be eaten (sit-down meal, buffet, breakfast, lunch, dinner, special occasion)?

Once the basics are established, **other points to consider** are:

- nutritional needs, including specific dietary needs
- time of year
- weather
- type of customer
- time available
- price
- portion control
- ability of the cook
- ability of the serving staff
- equipment available (for food preparation, cooking and serving)
- balance (colour, flavour, texture, shape, variety of ingredients)
- presentation (see Chapter 1.8).

Planning a good menu

Menu planning has strong links to the style of service offered.

Here are some tips:

- **Children's menus:** should be fun and include healthy alternatives to children's favourites, for example potato wedges instead of chips, served with a selection of naturally healthy vegetables such as peas and sweetcorn. Children could have more choice by offering smaller portions of main dishes from the adult menu.
- **Specials:** many restaurants have a 'specials board', which is a good way of adding seasonal dishes and offers to the menu.
- **Breakfast:** even simple breakfasts should offer a choice of hot (bacon, egg, sausage, tomato, etc.) and cold continental (rolls, croissants, cheese, cold meat, etc.) options. Hot and cold drinks and a tasty selection of preserves should be offered.
- **Lunch:** often needs to be served quickly for customers with limited time. Sandwiches, wraps and baguettes are ideal. An ideal menu will offer a variety of breads with a selection of hot and cold fillings, together with snack items such as jacket potatoes, salads, pasties, cakes, pastries and muffins. There should be something to appeal to everyone.
- **Evening meal:** vegetarian and healthy choices should be offered as well as dishes using a variety of cooking methods. In the UK, the most popular menus offer hot and cold starters, a variety of main courses and a selection of desserts that includes chocolate and fruit.

Choosing a menu

- Decide on the **main course** 'protein items' first, for example chicken breast, pork fillet, lamb cutlets, liver, cod, salmon, tuna, cheese, Quorn, tofu.
- Decide on the **desserts** – these should 'balance' the protein items for colour, flavour, texture and nutrients.
- Choose the **vegetables** – these should 'balance' other dishes chosen, especially with regard to colour.
- Choose the **starters**.

Types of menu

- **Table d'hôte** or set-price menu: a fixed- or set-price menu with a limited selection of dishes for every course.
- **A la carte menu:** all dishes are individually priced.
- **Party or function menu:** usually a fixed-price menu offered for parties or functions such as wedding receptions. Some party menus offer a limited choice.
- **Ethnic or speciality menu:** can be fixed-price or à la carte. Some offer dishes from particular countries, e.g. China or Italy, others offer specialised food, e.g. fish or vegetarian dishes.
- **Fast-food menu:** this is similar to a speciality menu. Food tends to have 'themes' such as burgers, chicken or baked potatoes. Items are priced separately.
- **Rotating menu cycle:** often used in primary schools. A fixed pattern of menus is used to cover a fixed number of days. The minimum number of days is eight, so that menus are never repeated on the same day each week.

Check your understanding
Tested

1 What are the 'four Ws' that need to be considered when menu planning?

2 Why is it important to have a range of colours and textures in a meal?

3 Why is it important to consider different dietary needs when planning a menu for a hotel restaurant?

4 What should a healthy two-course meal for a toddler contain?

5 What advice would you give to a teenager about healthy eating?

Exam tips

Questions on menu planning are often about the points that need to be considered when planning meals for a specific group of people (e.g. vegetarians). This includes menu planning alongside nutrition and healthy eating. The section on menu planning also has links to:
- food service, e.g. what foods could be offered for a buffet breakfast?
- health, safety and hygiene, e.g. why are high standards of hygiene and good temperature control important when preparing and serving meals to older people?

Revision Activity

Completed

Menus of ten need to be adapted to suit the dietary needs of customers. Look at the examples below that show how an original menu has been adapted for a vegetarian and a coeliac. Show how you would adapt the original menu for vegan and lactose intolerant customers.

Original menu

Beef Lasagne

Green Salad

Garlic Bread

Lemon Cheesecake

Adapted Menus

Vegetarian option

Vegetable Lasagne

Green Salad

Garlic Bread

Lemon Cheesecake

Coeliac (wheat intolerant)

Chilli Con Carne or

Ratatouille

Rice

Lemon crème brûlée

1.11 Portion Control and Costing

Key Facts

Good **portion control** is essential, in order to:

- ensure each customer gets the same size portion (avoid complaints)
- prevent waste
- make costing easier
- make ordering easier
- make a profit.

Ways of achieving portion control:

- cutting lines
- appropriate garnish or decoration denoting portions
- individual dishes
- weight of food before cooking, e.g. 100g fish fillet, 150g steak
- specific number of items, e.g. nine pieces of scampi, six chicken nuggets
- standard-sized equipment, e.g. ladles, spoons, scoops, glasses, dishes
- use of standard recipes.

Equipment used for portion control:

- individual dishes, tins, basins and moulds
- ladles, spoons and scoops
- glasses
- drink dispensers.

> **Exam tip**
>
> Good portion control is the key to having a profitable business. Questions in this section often refer to why portion control is needed, what equipment is used for portion control and how selling price is calculated.

Costing

When calculating costs and working out a selling price, the following need to be included:

- food costs (cost of ingredients needed to make a dish)
- overheads (gas, electricity, rates, rent, cost of equipment, etc.)
- staff wages (labour costs)
- profit
- VAT.

Computer resources (e.g. *The Nutrition Program* by Jenny Ridgwell) can be used to calculate the total cost of a recipe, cost per portion and a suggested selling price. The formula used to calculate selling price is:

$$\frac{\text{Cost per portion} \times 100}{40}$$

Round up the final cost so that the figure ends in a 5 or 0, e.g. £5.50 is a more realistic price than £5.47.

1.11 Portion Control and Costing

1 A chicken dish costs £2.40 per portion to make. Calculate the selling price using the formula.

2 Suggest ways of achieving good portion control.

3 Give the advantages of good portion control.

Revision Activity   Completed

Collect pictures of portioning equipment (from a catering catalogue or the internet). Make a set of work cards that matches equipment and the food it can be used to portion. A few examples are shown here to get you started.

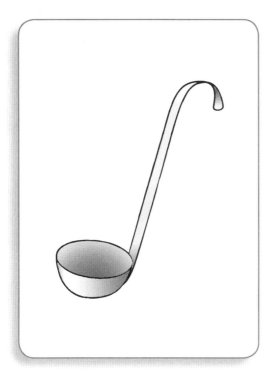

Ladle
Used for soups, gravies, sauces, etc.

Ice cream scoop
Used for ice cream, sorbets, frozen yogurt, mashed potatoes, etc.

1.12 Specialist Equipment

Key Facts ────────────────────────── Revised ☐

You need to be able to identify a range of specialist equipment used in the catering industry and to explain how to use safely and hygienically. Remember that specialist equipment can be used for catering or food service.

Catering

Hand equipment, e.g. knives
The basic knives used in every catering kitchen are:

- a cook's knife – for chopping
- a palette knife – for lifting, scraping and mixing
- a vegetable knife (sometimes called a paring knife) – for peeling and cutting small items of food
- a peeler – for peeling fruit and vegetables.

Safety rules for knives:

- Use the appropriate sized knife for the food to be cut.
- Keep knives sharp – a blunt knife is dangerous.
- Keep handles dry and grease free.
- Carry knives by the handle, blade downwards pointing towards the floor.
- Never try to catch a falling knife.
- Do not leave knives on the edge of chopping boards or table tops.
- Wash up carefully with sharp edge of blade facing away.
- Never place knives in washing up water where they cannot be seen.
- Store knives in a block or drawer.

Powered equipment
Ensure you know the use, care and maintenance of at least **one** piece of equipment from each of the following categories:

- **small** items such as electric mixers, microwaves and blenders
- **medium-sized** equipment such as potato chippers, floor-standing mixers and mincing machines
- **large-scale** equipment such as ovens, fryers, steamers and grills.

Food storage equipment
This includes:

- refrigerators, blast chillers, freezers and chill cabinets. Make sure you know the key temperatures.

Food service

Hand equipment
This includes:

- crockery, cutlery, table linen and glassware (used for table-laying)
- serving equipment such as ice buckets, bottle openers, carafes, serving platters, tongs.

Powered equipment
This includes:

- coffee machines, toasters, flambé trolleys, credit or debit card payment facilities, hot and cold service counters.

> **Exam tip**
>
> Learn the correct names and uses of pieces of equipment you use in your practical sessions. When you revise the use of knives and other equipment also revise the first-aid treatment for cuts, burns, scalds and falls.

Check your understanding

Tested

1 Identify the following pieces of equipment.

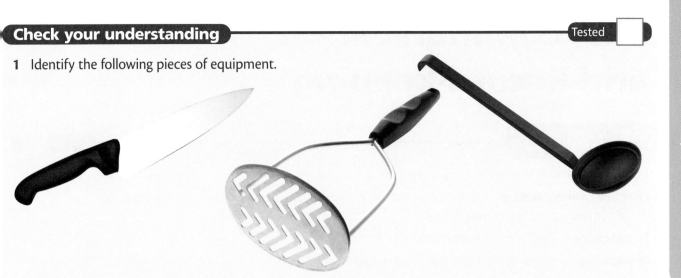

2 A set of knives should last a lifetime. What advice would you give to a young chef buying a set of knives?

3 Name and give a use for two knives that you think are essential in a catering kitchen.

4 Give four safety rules a chef should follow when using knives.

5 Explain the importance of efficient refrigerators and freezers in a catering kitchen.

6 Evaluate the use of a microwave in a fast-food outlet.

Revision Activity

Completed

Choose three pieces of equipment you use regularly in your practical lessons. Prepare a series of work cards showing a picture of the equipment on one side and the use, safety and cleaning points on the other. Here is an example to get you started.

Microwave cooker

Use: Microwave ovens cook by producing energy waves which 'agitate' the molecules in food. This causes friction, which in turn heats the food. They cook food quicker than conventional ovens. They are often used to defrost, reheat and cook food.

Safety and cleaning: do not use if door seal is damaged. Do not use metal containers. Clean up spillages straight away.

1.13 Communication and Record-keeping

Key Facts

Communication

Effective communication is important in the catering industry. This is because it is a 'service' industry. Good communication is a combination of:

- **observing** – watching customers and offering help and advice
- **listening** – listening carefully to what is being said
- **thinking** – thinking carefully about what to say using commonly used words, not jargon
- **knowing** – what your establishment offers
- **describing** – e.g. describing items on a menu, the services provided by your establishment
- **suggesting** – e.g. food, wine, alternatives, places to visit.

There are different **types of communication**. These include:

- verbal
- non-verbal (unspoken: for example body language)
- written
- telephone
- fax
- ICT – internet, email, web.

Different types of communication are needed for different circumstances. Some customers may have communication or mobility difficulties, for example, they may be partially sighted or blind, deaf or hard of hearing, have speech difficulties or be a wheelchair user. Other customers with particular needs are those eating on their own, older people and the very young and children. A catering and hospitality business cannot exist without customers. The main purpose of staff employed in the hospitality industry is to look after customers' needs. Good communication means successful businesses and happy customers.

ICT is used extensively throughout the catering industry. Many catering establishments rely heavily on computer systems for communication, record-keeping and planning.

You need to know about at least three of the following uses of ICT:

- **Reservation systems:** run by hotel groups. A customer can ring or email a central reservation number or email address and a room can be booked for any hotel in the group (either in the UK or abroad).
- **Management systems:** room reservations, guest billing, guest history.
- **Electronic Point of Sale (EPOS):** a number of machines are linked to a central computer. Guests can order from the bar, restaurant and shop and all transactions are passed to the central computer for bills to be generated automatically.
- **Stock control systems:** these hold details of suppliers. They generate orders automatically when stock levels fall, give a detailed record of stock issued and current prices of stock held.
- **Food and beverage management systems:** this is a database of recipes, quantities needed, ingredient codes, tax codes and other information used for functions.
- **Events management:** computers are used extensively when planning, organising and running large events, e.g. wedding receptions, banquets and conferences. The data used to plan and organise one event can be stored and used when planning similar future events.

- **Menu engineering:** chefs can create 'perfect' menus in terms of popularity and profit.
- **Dietary analysis:** there are many nutritional analysis programs, particularly for use with people on special diets such as hospital patients, where an accurate record of a patient's diet is needed. Large companies like McDonald's issue detailed nutritional content of their dishes for consumers.

Record-keeping

It is important to keep accurate, appropriate records. The types of records used in the catering industry are:

- stock control sheets
- invoices
- staff rotas
- food and drink orders
- restaurant bookings
- details of accidents.

Check your understanding

Tested

1 Why is it important for a storekeeper to keep accurate records?

2 What type of communication would you suggest for: making a restaurant booking; placing a food order to a regular supplier; finding out about a holiday hotel?

3 State three pieces of information that should be recorded in an accident book.

4 Explain the importance of ICT in the catering industry.

Exam tip

Communication and record-keeping are important areas in the catering industry. Learn the main types of communication and make sure you know how ICT is used in the industry.

Revision Activity

Completed

With a friend or family member, practise answering a telephone call and taking a restaurant booking so that you remember what important points need to be recorded. For example, the customer's name, contact details, day, date and time of booking, number of guests expected, any specific needs (lack of mobility, specific dietary needs), etc.

1.14 Environmental Issues

Key Facts
Revised

Remember the 'three Rs' – **reduce**, **reuse**, **recycle**.

Reduce waste:
- Store food correctly.
- Handle food correctly.
- Do not prepare too much food.
- Have accurate portion control.
- Recycle where possible.
- Use dispensers for salt, sugar, sauces, etc.
- Review waste procedures regularly.

Conserve energy and water:
- Invest in energy-efficient equipment.
- Keep lids on pans.
- Keep equipment clean.
- Have regular maintenance checks.
- Have efficient temperature control.
- Have full loads for washing machines and dishwashers.
- Turn equipment off when not in use.

Check your understanding
Tested

1 Explain why catering establishments may have an environmental policy.

2 What are the main energy-saving tips you would recommend to a restaurant?

3 Explain the terms biodegradable and recyclable.

Exam tips

Make sure you know what the term 'the three Rs' means.

During your practical sessions, practise ways of:
- saving energy, e.g. put lids on pans, never put hot food in the fridge
- saving water, e.g. use the correct amount of water for cooking and washing up
- minimising waste, e.g. store and handle food correctly, use oldest food first.

Use this knowledge when answering questions on environmental issues.

Revision Activity
Completed

Make a work card like the one here and fill in as many points as you can under the 'three Rs'.

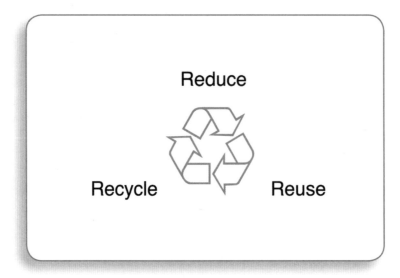

Key Facts

The main reasons for **packaging food** are to:

- protect the contents
- keep food fresh
- make food easier to handle and transport
- improve hygiene
- make contents look attractive
- give information on contents, storage and use.

The main packaging materials used are:

- paper and card – easily printed, lightweight, recyclable but weak when wet
- glass – easily printed, recyclable, can carry liquids but easily broken
- modified atmosphere packaging (MAP) – gives foods like salads a longer shelf life but once the pack is opened, food will go off quickly
- metal (cans) – recyclable, strong, rigid – but must be coated inside to prevent reaction with food and is expensive to produce
- plastic and polystyrene – strong, flexible, lightweight but not easily recycled.

Packaged food

Pre-prepared foods are widely used throughout the hospitality and catering industries. They include such things as bread, cakes, biscuits, pastries and pies that may only need heating or portioning, and other pre-prepared foods that have a longer shelf life and require regeneration or cooking before they can be used. These pre-prepared foods include cook-chill products, frozen foods, dried food and mixes, canned foods, vacuum packaging, part-baked products and fresh foods such as washed salad items and vegetables.

As a caterer it is important to understand packaging labels so that you can inform staff and customers of the contents of the dishes you produce and maintain safety, hygiene and quality standards.

What's on a label?

Look at the following diagram that explains what's on a label.

Make sure you know how important it is to know what's in food – particularly for customers with special dietary needs, food allergies or intolerances.

What's on a label?

Product name, Product description
Manufacturer's name and address
Ingredients list (in order – heaviest first)
Weight
Storage instructions, cooking instructions
Nutrition information
Batch number, Bar code
Special claims, e.g. low fat
Specific warnings, e.g. may contain nuts
Display until or 'use by' dates

Check your understanding

1 Match the following foods to their recommended packaging:

Polystyrene box	Sweet and sour pork
Flat, cardboard box	French fries
Foil container with card lid	Burger
Clear triangular plastic box	Chicken biryani
Cardboard cone	Pizza
Plastic container with lid	BLT sandwich

Exam tips

You may have had a take-away meal or been to a fast-food restaurant. Think about the different types of packaging used. For example, cardboard boxes for pizzas, polystyrene boxes for kebabs, fish and chips and burgers, plastic boxes with tight fitting lids for Chinese or Indian food, cardboard cones for chips (French fries), polystyrene or rigid card cups with lids for hot drinks.

Why are these materials used? Think about keeping food hot or cold, keeping in shape, being light to carry, preventing leaks, etc.

Questions on packaging may relate to types of packaging, the reasons for their use or the information that can be found on the packaging label.

Revision Activity

Completed

Prepare work cards to illustrate packaging materials and their uses.
An example has been done for you.

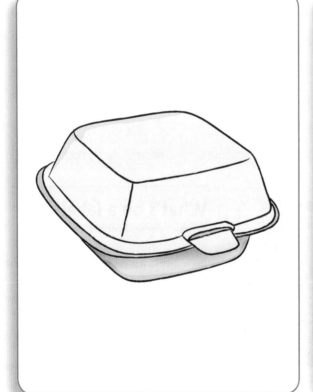

Polystyrene boxes

Used for: burgers, fish and chips, kebabs, etc.

Advantages: strong, lightweight, easy to print, do not react with food, act as an insulator to keep food hot

Disadvantages: not very environmentally friendly

2.2 Catering Controlled Assessments

The practical tasks are designed so that you can demonstrate the following range of skills:

● research and planning skills

● practical skills

● an ability to evaluate work and suggest improvements.

For both Task 1 and Task 2 you will need to carry out research, so that you make an informed choice of dishes for the practical part of the assessment.

There is a page limit of 4 pages (8 sides) of A4 for Task 1.

There is a page limit of 10 pages (20 sides) of A4 for Task 2.

Tips for the Controlled Assessments

Research
Research can be carried out in a variety of ways.

Primary research is the most valuable type of research and can be carried out by visiting a supermarket or restaurant, watching demonstrations, taking part in tasting sessions, carrying out questionnaires or surveys and trialling recipes.

Secondary research is taken from the internet, recipe books, text books, TV, radio, magazines, newspapers and leaflets. It is not worth as many marks as primary research.

For Task 2, any first-hand experience (for example, of international cuisine) that can be included in the research will make it much more interesting and relevant.

Planning
You should choose dishes that will enable you to:

● answer the task

● demonstrate a range of practical skills

● demonstrate your confidence and competence in making

● demonstrate presentation skills

● demonstrate dove-tailing of tasks, i.e. fitting tasks together so that when one dish is cooking/cooling you get on with another task – for Task 2

● demonstrate a knowledge of nutrition, cost and menu planning.

Writing an order of work
Using a colour-coded method of writing an order of work will ensure that all the main points are included.
Here is how to do it:

● Word process the recipe and method for each dish (shorten if lengthy but keep main points).

● Make sure the method is typed with spaces between each step.

● Enlarge recipes (minimum font size 14).

● Print out each recipe onto different coloured card or paper.

● Cut up each stage of each recipe.

- Take a sheet of A3 paper and divide into three.

- In the centre column, write down all the tasks from each recipe that can be done in mise-en-place time.

- Continue the centre column by assembling tasks like a jigsaw puzzle in the most logical way.

- Remember that dishes needing the longest cooking time, cooling time or setting time need to be made first. Hot food needs to be served hot, so as a general rule accompaniments like vegetables need to be cooked towards the end of the test. Desserts are often made first.

- Main dishes should be scheduled so that they come out of the oven at the end of the test or, in the case of steaks and similar foods, are cooked at the end of the test so that they can be served hot without the need for 'hot-holding'. Check sequencing and ensure all food can be cooked in the time available.

- Fill in the first column with times.

- Use the final column to add special points on health, safety and hygiene plus all cooking temperatures and times.

Example 1: colour coded order of work showing sequencing of two recipes
Recipes printed on different-coloured card

Vegetable Lasagne

Recipe:
2 onions
2 courgettes
1 red pepper or 1 aubergine
1 vegetable stock cube
1 tin chopped tomatoes
1–2 tbs tomato purée
½ teaspoon mixed herbs
Lasagne sheets

Cheese sauce:
50g marg
50g flour
500mls milk
100–150g grated cheese

Method:

1. Chop, dice or slice all vegetables into even sized pieces.

2. Place all vegetables in a large pan with the tin of tomatoes, stock cube, 125mls water, herbs and tomato purée.

3. Bring to boil and then simmer gently for approximately 20–30 minutes. Check seasoning.

4. Make cheese sauce, melt margarine, add flour and add milk a little at a time! Bring to boil stirring all the time. Remove from heat and stir in cheese.

5. Assemble lasagne – put a spoonful of cheese sauce on base, then a layer of lasagne sheets, a spoonful of vegetable sauce, etc. Finish with lasagne sheets and pour remainder of cheese sauce all over the top.

6. Bake for approximately 30 minutes at Gas mark 5 or 180°C.

Chocolate Roulade

Roulade:
3 eggs
75g (3oz) caster sugar
60g SR flour (1½ tbs)
15g cocoa powder (1 level tbs)

Filling:
250mls double or whipping cream
200g raspberries

Decoration:
chocolate leaves, whipped cream, fruit coulis

Method:

1. Grease and line a large Swiss roll tin with greaseproof paper. Light oven Gas mark 6 or 200°C. Weigh out all ingredients accurately (place eggs and sugar in bowl and place flour and cocoa powder in a sieve standing on a metal plate).

2. Whisk eggs and sugar until the mixture looks like a thick foam and is so stiff it leaves the trail of the whisk. Carefully fold in the sieved flour and cocoa with a palette knife.

3. Pour into the Swiss roll tin and tilt tin so that mixture spreads evenly. Bake for 10–12 minutes until just set and springy to touch.

4. Remove from oven and turn out onto a sheet of lightly sugared greaseproof paper. Trim off all edges, then roll up quickly and allow to cool.

5. When cool, unroll gently, spread generously with cream or cream and raspberries and then re-roll.

6. Decorate top of roulade with piped cream and chocolate shapes (if wanted) or serve on decorated plates.

Recipes (lists of ingredients) cut off each card

Vegetable Lasagne

Recipe:
2 onions
2 courgettes
1 red pepper or 1 aubergine
1 vegetable stock cube
1 tin chopped tomatoes
1–2 tbs tomato purée
½ teaspoon mixed herbs
Lasagne sheets

Cheese sauce:
50g marg
50g flour
500mls milk
100–150g grated cheese

Chocolate Roulade

Roulade:
3 eggs
75g (3oz) caster sugar
60g SR flour (1½ tbs)
15g cocoa powder (1 level tbs)

Filling:
250mls double or whipping cream
200g raspberries

Decoration:
chocolate leaves, whipped cream, fruit coulis

Methods cut up and arranged in logical order

1. Grease and line a large Swiss roll tin with greaseproof paper. Light oven Gas mark 6 or 200°C. Weigh out all ingredients accurately (place eggs and sugar in bowl and place flour and cocoa powder in a sieve standing on a metal plate).

1. Chop, dice or slice all vegetables into even sized pieces.

2. Place all vegetables in a large pan with the tin of tomatoes, stock cube, 125mls water, herbs and tomato purée.

3. Bring to boil and then simmer gently for approx 20–30 mins. Check seasoning.

2. Whisk eggs and sugar until the mixture looks like a thick foam and is so stiff it leaves the trail of the whisk. Carefully fold in the sieved flour and cocoa with a palette knife.

3. Pour into the Swiss roll tin and tilt tin so that mixture spreads evenly. Bake for 10–12 minutes until just set and springy to touch.

4. Make cheese sauce, melt margarine, add flour and add milk a little at a time! Bring to boil stirring all the time. Remove from heat and stir in cheese.

4. Remove from oven and turn out onto a sheet of lightly sugared greaseproof paper. Trim off all edges, then roll up quickly and allow to cool.

5. Assemble lasagne – put a spoonful of cheese sauce on base, then a layer of lasagne sheets, a spoonful of vegetable sauce, etc. Finish with lasagne sheets and pour remainder of cheese sauce all over the top.

6. Bake for approximately 30 minutes at Gas mark 5 or 180°C.

5. When cool, unroll gently, spread generously with cream or cream and raspberries and then re-roll.

6. Decorate top of roulade with piped cream and chocolate shapes (if wanted) or serve on decorated plates.

Order of work ready to add timing and special points columns

See example 2 for a completed order of work.

Vegetable Lasagne

Recipe:

2 onions
2 courgettes
1 red pepper or 1 aubergine
1 vegetable stock cube
1 tin chopped tomatoes
1–2 tbs tomato purée
½ teaspoon mixed herbs
Lasagne sheets

Cheese sauce:

50g marg
50g flour
500mls milk
100–150g grated cheese

Method:

1. Chop, dice or slice all vegetables into even sized pieces.

2. Place all vegetables in a large pan with the tin of tomatoes, stock cube, 125mls water, herbs and tomato purée.

3. Bring to boil and then simmer gently for approximately 20–30 minutes. Check seasoning.

4. Make cheese sauce, melt margarine, add flour and add milk a little at a time! Bring to boil stirring all the time. Remove from heat and stir in cheese.

5. Assemble lasagne – put a spoonful of cheese sauce on base, then a layer of lasagne sheets, a spoonful of vegetable sauce, etc. Finish with lasagne sheets and pour remainder of cheese sauce all over the top.

6. Bake for approximately 30 minutes at Gas mark 5 or 180°C.

Cashew Nut Paella

2 tbs olive oil
25g butter or margarine
1 red onion (chopped)
150g Arborio (risotto) rice
1 teaspoon ground turmeric
1 teaspoon ground cumin
½ teaspoon chilli powder
3 garlic cloves (crushed)
1 green chilli (sliced)

1 green pepper (diced)
1 red pepper (diced)
75g baby corn cobs (sliced in half lengthways)
2 tbs pitted black olives
1 large tomato (seeded and diced)
450ml vegetable stock (1 stock cube)
75g unsalted cashew nuts
25g frozen peas
2 tbs chopped parsley and pinch cayenne pepper

1. Gently heat olive oil and butter in large pan. Add chopped onion and sauté for a few minutes until the onion has softened.

2. Stir in the rice, spices, peppers, baby corn, olives and tomato and cook over a medium heat for 1 to 2 minutes.

3. Pour over the stock and bring the mixture to the boil. Reduce the heat and cook for approximately 20 minutes, stirring.

4. Add the cashew nuts and peas to the mixture and cook for a further 5 minutes, stirring occasionally.

5. Sprinkle with chopped parsley and cayenne pepper.

6. Serve immediately.

Bread Rolls

350g strong bread flour or plain flour + a little extra (for kneading)
1 sachet of quick acting yeast
15g marg
½ level tsp salt
175 mls 'hand hot' water
1 tbsp poppy or sesame seeds or rolled oats – optional

1. Sieve flour into mixing bowl. Add salt and rub in margarine. Add the dried yeast.

2. Add the measured amount of water *all at once*. Have extra water in a jug in case it is needed as the mixture must be slightly wet at this stage.

3. Mix well to a *soft* dough and turn out onto floured surface.

4. Knead for 5–10 minutes until dough is smooth and stretchy. Allow dough to rest for as long as possible. (Wash up your bowl at this stage and grease baking tray).

5. 'Knock back' dough (re-knead) to original size. Cut into 6 - 8 even sized pieces.

6. Shape into the various rolls and place on a greased baking tray.

7. LEAVE TO PROVE (RISE) for 15–30 minutes or until doubled in size.

8. Bake in preheated oven Gas No 6–7 or 200°C for 15–20 minutes, until rolls are golden brown and 'sound' hollow when tapped. Cool on wire rack.

Normandy Apple Flan

Pate sucre
150g plain flour
100g block marg or butter
1 tbs caster sugar
1 egg yolk
3–4 small eating apples

75g soft marg
75g caster sugar
1 egg
1–2 tablespoons milk
75g ground almonds
15g (1 level tablespoon) S.R. or plain flour

1. For pastry – rub fat into flour.

2. Add egg yolk, which has been beaten together with caster sugar and form into a dough using a fork. Chill for 20 minutes.

3. Use pastry to line flan dish.

4. Cream marg and sugar till light in colour and fluffy. Add beaten egg. Stir in almonds and flour. Mix lightly.

5. Peel and core the apples. Cut each apple in half.

6. Place apple halves evenly around the pastry case.

7. Spread the almond mixture evenly over the apples.

8. Bake gas 5 – 180°C for at least 20–25 minutes until pastry case is golden and almond mixture is 'springy' to the touch.

Variation:
Use pears instead of apples.

Colour coded order of work

Example 2 has been done in exactly the same way as example 1, using four recipes instead of two. Timings and special points have been added to show how an order of work should be completed. Please note that there is a different colour for each recipe. The extra colour has been added to show mise-en-place and washing up sessions.

Time	Order of work	Special points
9.00	Mise-en-place: • Prepare self, sanitise work unit, collect cooking equipment and serving dishes, lay serving table, weigh ingredients. • Rub in for paté sucre. Rub in for bread dough. Chop vegetables for lasagne and paella. Wash salad ingredients. Scald milk for roux sauce. Make stock and crush garlic for paella, grate cheese, make salad dressing and prepare garnishes.	High standards of personal and kitchen hygiene. Refrigerate all perishables. Cover food. Preheat oven Gas mark 5.
9.30	Add egg yolk and sugar to rubbed up pastry mixture and form dough. Chill.	20 minutes in fridge.
9.35	Add hand hot water to rubbed-in bread mixture. Mix to a soft dough. Knead for at least 5 minutes.	Check temperature of water carefully. Add water all at once.
9.50	Wash up.	
9.55	Make almond filling for flan – cream margarine and sugar, add egg, stir in almonds and flour.	Check mixture is a dropping consistency.
10.05	Roll out pastry and line loose bottomed flan dish.	Crimp edges of pastry to neaten.
10.15	Peel and core apples – cut each one in half, place round pastry case. Spread almond mixture evenly over apples. Bake.	Gas mark 5 for 20–25 minutes.
10.25	Knock back bread dough. Cut into eight even sized pieces and shape. Place on greased tray.	Shape as knots and plaits.
10.40	Place chopped vegetables for lasagne in pan with tin tomatoes, stock cube, water, herbs and purée. Bring to boil, then reduce heat and simmer.	High heat to start, then reduce heat and simmer for 20 minutes.
10.45	Prepare paella – gently heat olive oil and butter in pan and sauté chopped onion. Turn off heat once cooked.	Sauté onion for 5 minutes over LOW heat to soften but not brown.
10.50	Check Normandy Apple Flan. Remove from oven if cooked and allow to cool.	Centre should be brown and springy.
10.55	Make cheese sauce – melt margarine, add flour, cook roux, add warm milk a little at a time. Bring to boil, take off heat and add cheese.	Stir ALL the time. Add milk OFF heat.
11.10	Assemble lasagne – cheese sauce on base, then lasagne sheets, then vegetable sauce. Finish with lasagne sheets and pour over remaining cheese sauce. Bake.	Increase oven heat to Gas mark 6. Bake lasagne for 30 minutes.
11.10	Bake bread rolls.	Top shelf – 20 minutes.
11.20	Finish paella – add rice, spices, peppers, baby corn, olives and tomato to onion. Cook for 2 minutes.	Medium heat.

11.25	Pour over stock and bring to boil. Reduce heat and cook for 20 minutes.	Stir occasionally. Low to medium heat.
11.30	Wash up.	
11.35	Make salad – wash and dry lettuce, peel and slice cucumber, wash and halve baby tomatoes, wash and slice celery, wash and slice radish, wash and chop pepper. Place in bowl.	Refrigerate until needed.
11.40	Check bread rolls. Cool on wire rack.	Base should sound hollow when tapped.
11. 45	Remove Normandy Apple Flan from flan ring and place on plate.	Use oven gloves.
11.50	Add cashew nuts and peas to paella and cook for further 5 minutes.	Stir occasionally.
11.50	Check lasagne – turn off oven.	Will retain heat.
11.55	Place bread rolls in basket, add butter dish. Serve salad with jug of dressing. Place paella in warmed serving dish. Remove lasagne from oven. Garnish remaining dishes.	Clean edges of all dishes. Add garnishes.
12.00	Present all dishes.	Final clearing up.

Carrying out the task

In order to gain high marks in this section, you must demonstrate:

- high standards of personal hygiene, e.g. wearing of apron/whites, hair back, no nail varnish, no jewellery, etc.
- good personal hygiene habits, e.g. no licking fingers, always taste with a clean teaspoon, etc.
- safe use of equipment, especially knives, pans and electrical equipment
- selection of correct tools, e.g. correct size of knife for chopping
- the use of a wide variety of commodities within the task chosen
- good food hygiene, e.g. perishable foods refrigerated and not left on work unit/table, using a temperature probe to ensure food is cooked
- neat, organised work
- safe use of oven and hob
- working to time
- independent working
- good technical skills
- little food waste
- logical sequence of work, e.g. food that needs to be cooked for a long time, be set or served cold needs to be made first
- wide variety of skills
- high standard of final presentation, e.g. portion control, use of garnish and decoration, good colour, correct temperature, correct texture, good flavour, appropriate serving dishes.

Evaluating the task

In order to gain high marks in this section, you need to discuss:

- the task as a whole including the success and/or suitability of research
- the suitability of dishes/menu chosen

- any changes you would make to the choice of dishes with reasons
- how customers would regard the dishes in terms of appearance, flavour and texture – would customers be prepared to pay for the dishes?
- any improvements you would make, with your reasons
- the size and cost per portion (see Chapter 3.5 on portion control and costing)
- a suggested selling price per portion (for Task 2)
- the nutritional content of the meal with valid comments (for Task 2).

Use the coursework checklist below to ensure you do not miss out any stages.

Table 2.2.1 Coursework checklist

Stages	What to include	✔
Analysis	<ul><li>Brief in your own words</li><li>Brain storm (thought shower) ideas of where, how and what you will research</li></ul>	
Research	Use as many of these ways as you can:<ul><li>Interviews</li><li>Surveys</li><li>Questionnaires</li><li>Internet research</li><li>Other media resources, e.g. TV, video, magazines, leaflets</li><li>Demonstrations and talks</li><li>Displays</li><li>Tasting sessions</li><li>Visits</li><li>Letters or emails to industry, companies</li><li>Recipe trialling</li></ul>	
Analysis of research	<ul><li>What you did</li><li>What you have found out (include photographs, graphs and tables)</li><li>How you will use your findings</li></ul>	
Choice and reasons for practical session	<ul><li>Summary of research</li><li>Final specification in your own words</li><li>Choice of dishes (written in menu order for a meal)</li><li>Reasons for choice</li><li>Order of work – include hygiene and safety points and portion control</li><li>Shopping list</li><li>Equipment list (if appropriate)</li></ul>	
Evaluation	Written comments on:<ul><li>Success of research</li><li>Suitability of dishes for the task</li><li>Customer acceptability in terms of appearance, flavour and texture</li><li>Improvements that could be made to choice, planning and making</li></ul>	
Costing	<ul><li>Calculation of cost per portion</li><li>Written comments on size and cost per portion</li></ul>For Task 2:<ul><li>Suggested selling price with justification</li></ul>	
Nutritional analysis	For Task 2:<ul><li>A nutritional analysis of dishes (use a computer program or food tables)</li><li>Written comments on the nutritional analysis showing how meal could be improved or modified with justification</li></ul>	

3.1 The Hospitality Industry

🔍 Key Facts

- Hospitality establishments provide accommodation, food and/or drink.
- Hospitality establishments may be commercial (profit making) or non-commercial (catering services, non-profit making).
- Contract caterers provide food and drink for organisations such as businesses, prisons, schools, universities and hospitals, where accommodation is not the main focus.
- Hospitality is the fastest growing industry in the UK.
- Hospitality has important links with tourism because people travel for work or pleasure and require accommodation, food and drink.
- Hospitality has important links with entertainment and leisure.

The **main sectors** of the hospitality industry are:

- **accommodation**, e.g. hotels and guest houses
- **food and drink**, e.g. cafes and restaurants
- **meetings and events**, e.g. hotels and conference centres
- **entertainment and leisure**, e.g. spa centres and golf clubs
- **travel and tourism**, e.g. aeroplanes, cruise ships and hotels.

Staff can be:

- **full time**
- **part time**
- **casual** or **seasonal**.

Check your understanding

1 List three types of establishment you would expect to find in the entertainment and leisure sector of the hospitality industry.

2 Explain why a hotel situated in a British seaside resort may employ a mixture of full-time, part-time and casual staff.

Exam tip

Questions often relate to the link between hospitality, tourism, leisure and entertainment and the type of staff that are employed in the industry.

Revision Activity

Completed ☐

Make a chart like the one below. The first two are examples to get you started.

Outlet	Sectors they provide for	Links to tourism
McDonald's	Food and beverages. Children's parties.	Tourists may visit for food and drink. Known worldwide.
Boarding School	Food and beverages. Accommodation for teachers and students.	Students may be from abroad.
Sea View Hotel		
Caravan Park		
Leisure Centre		
Luigi's Restaurant		
Guest House		
Wine Bar		
Conference Centre		

3.2 Types of Service and Client Groups

Key Facts

The **types of service** that the hospitality industry provides include:

● accommodation
● food and drink
● conference facilities, e.g. business conference
● function facilities, e.g. wedding reception in a church hall.

Accommodation

Customers may need accommodation for one or more nights. Accommodation can be in basic single, twin or double rooms with en suite facilities or in a more luxurious room or suite. The cost will depend upon the facilities, the geographical location and the level of service.

Food and drink

Customers may need full meals for breakfast, lunch and dinner. Meals may be from a set menu, table d'hôte or à la carte menu. Breakfast may be continental, full English or 'mix and match' and is often served buffet style. Some establishments have special 'meal deals' where customers get the cheapest meal free. Many establishments offer children's meals at a reduced price. Some establishments may have a snack menu, usually in the bar, where customers can order snacks rather than meals. Delegates at a business conference and guests at a wedding reception often have pre-arranged set menus. Delegates at a business conference may require drinks and snacks at specific times during the day. Sometimes these are self-service and available all day.

Conference facilities

Rooms for a conference can be laid out in a number of styles. The main styles are:

● **theatre** – rows of seats so that all delegates can watch a presentation or listen to a speaker/presenter
● **boardroom** – a large table (rectangular, oval or round) where all delegates can see one another
● **cabaret** – lots of small tables for groups of delegates to work together
● **top table** – the most important people sit on the top table facing everyone else (this is often used at wedding receptions).

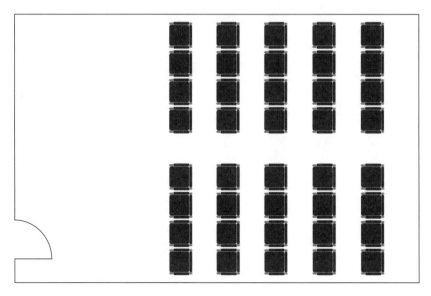

theatre

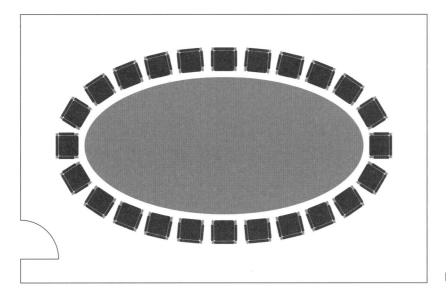

Boardroom

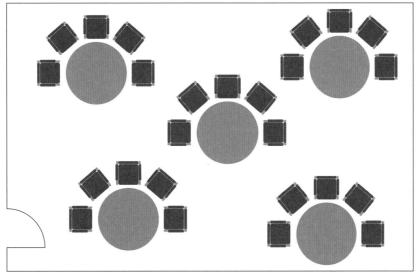

cabaret

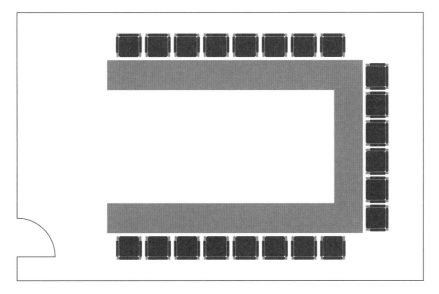

Top table

Function facilities

Customers may need a venue to hold a function such as a wedding reception or birthday party. Many establishments offer these facilities, e.g. church halls, public houses, civic centres, historic houses, restaurants and hotels. Costs will include the hire of the room and other requirements. Customers often want to provide their own food, drink and entertainment such as music. Some establishments allow this; others do not.

To help you revise this topic, study the two charts that show different functions common to the hospitality industry.

Equipment
- Flip charts and pens
- Computer equipment
- Projector and screen
- Audio equipment
- Delegate packs (paper, pens)
- Promotional material
- Internet access (Wi-Fi or cable)

Meeting Rooms
- Main meeting room
- Style of layout (boardroom, theatre, cabaret, top table)
- Syndicate rooms

Needs of Delegates at a Conference

Is there anything else you could add?

For example: guests with special needs, cost, etc.

Food and Drink
- Breakfast
- Lunch, dinner
- Snacks
- Teas and coffees
- Timings (agreed with organiser)
- Location (refreshments served in or out of conference room)
- Type of service
- Menu
- Water, juices and sweets for tables in meeting rooms

Accommodation
- Type of room
- En-suite facilities
- Type of occupancy
- Wi-Fi, TV, radio, DVD
- Car parking for delegates
- Leisure facilities

Function Room

- Layout of table and chairs
- Buffet/serving tables
- Space for serving food
- Space for bar if needed
- Space for dancing?
- Space for disco/group?

Equipment and Décor

- Audio and visual equipment
- Appropriate colour scheme
- Table linen, crockery, cutlery and glasses
- Decorations, e.g. flowers, table confetti
- Cake stand
- Seating plan, place name cards, favours,
- Cleaning material and equipment to clean hall at the end

Needs of guests at Wedding Reception in Church Hall.

Is there anything else you could add?

For example: car parking, disabled access, etc.

Food and Drink

- Menu (are there cooking/heating/storage facilities?)
- Type of service (buffet or table service)
- Timings (of food and speeches)
- Drinks, e.g. alcoholic and non-alcoholic
- Champagne reception?
- Drinks for speeches and cutting cake

Accommodation

- No overnight accommodation available
- Area required for coats (cloakroom)
- Toilet facilities

The **types of client** that the hospitality industry cater for include:

● **businesses** – commercial (profit making) businesses and organisations
● **private clients** – non-commercial (non-profit making) individuals
● **different age groups**, e.g. children, teenagers, adults, older people or mixed age groups of tourists, club members, etc.

Check your understanding

Tested

1 Discuss the main points you would need to consider when planning a tea party for a group of senior citizens in a day centre.

2 A manager has requested a meeting room for ten delegates with a boardroom layout.
   Draw the layout and suggest what else the delegates will need.

Exam tip

Questions on this section often relate to event planning. It is important to know the different client groups and the types of service provided by the hospitality industry.

Revision Activity

Completed

Using the information given in the charts above, prepare your own chart to show the needs of a client who wants to hold a dinner party for 12 guests in their own home. The headings are provided but you will need to draw larger boxes.

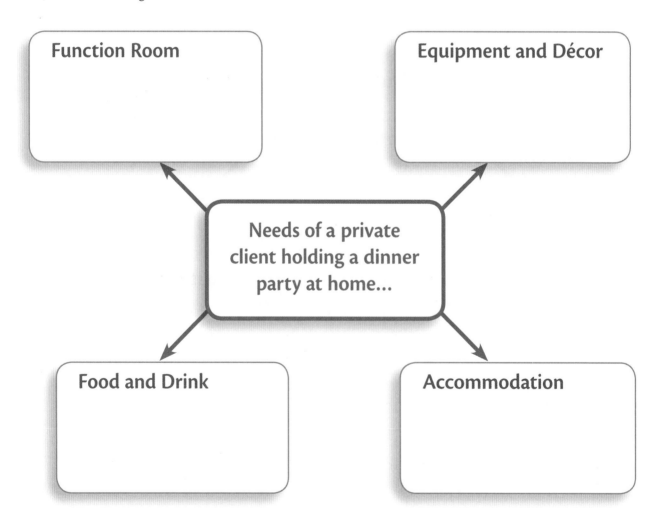

Function Room

Equipment and Décor

Needs of a private client holding a dinner party at home...

Food and Drink

Accommodation

3.3 Job Roles, Employment and Training

Key Facts

Revised

Jobs in the hospitality industry are found in the following areas:

- **management**, e.g. Hotel Manager, Accountant
- **front office** (also known as Front of House or Reception), e.g. receptionist, porter, concierge, administrative staff, e.g. cashier
- **accommodation**, e.g. housekeeper, maintenance officer
- **conference managers**, e.g. conference and banqueting manager in a large hotel.

Jobs can be at the following levels:

- **management** – Hotel Manager or Assistant Manager and in large establishments staff who are in charge of major departments, e.g. Reception Manager, Conference and Banqueting Manager
- **supervisory** – Head Housekeeper, Head Receptionist
- **operative** – housekeeper, porter, conference and banqueting wait staff.

Staff can be:

- **full time**
- **part time**
- **casual** or **seasonal**.

Training

There are employment opportunities at every level in the hospitality industry – for school leavers with no formal training through to those with university degrees. Many establishments offer 'training on the job' or send employees on day-release/college courses.

Check your understanding

Tested

1 Give five qualities needed by a receptionist working in a five-star hotel.

2 Explain the role of a night porter.

3 State two occasions when casual staff may be employed by a hotel.

> **Exam tip**
>
> There are often short questions about the roles and responsibilities of staff who work in the hospitality industry at the beginning of the examination paper. Make sure you know the types of jobs available in the different departments.

Fill in the charts below, showing the operating levels and responsibilities of key staff who work in the hospitality industry.

Table 3.3.1

Job role (front office)	Operating level	Responsibilities
Head receptionist		
Assistant receptionist		
Porter		

Table 3.3.2

Job role (conference and banqueting)	Operating level	Responsibilities
Conference and banqueting manager		
Station head waiter		
Banqueting wait staff		

3.4 Planning for Functions and Events

 Key Facts

When planning a function or event, the following are the most important points to consider:

- **date and time of event** (term time, daytime, evening?)
- **choice of venue** (on or off site, with/without cooking or reheating facilities)
- **cost, portion control and profit** (profit may not be applicable for all events)
- **advertising and promotion** (invitations, posters, flyers)
- **number of guests** (must be a minimum of ten)
- **type of menu** (buffet, sit-down meal, etc.)
- **dishes chosen** (consider specific dietary needs)
- **style of service** (self-service, assisted service, wait service)
- **décor and room layout** (colour scheme, decorations, flowers, dance space, buffet or sit-down style, layout of tables and chairs)
- **table layout** (place setting, style of napkin fold, table decorations)
- **menu cards and place names** (to match theme, décor, invitations, etc.)
- **risk assessment** (safety, hygiene, fire, first aid)
- **staffing** (reception, kitchen, food service, housekeeping).

Check your understanding

1 Stan and Joan are holding a party to celebrate their golden wedding anniversary and have invited 50 guests including family and friends. Suggest how the room and tables could be decorated for the party and the type of food service you would recommend.

2 Explain the importance of good communication between Stan and Joan and the party organiser.

Exam tips

Planning, organising and running an event is the main focus of Hospitality and Catering Unit 4. It is likely that there will be at least one question on some aspect of event planning in the examination.

Think carefully about all the tasks you (and your team) had to carry out in order to have a successful event. The success of your event will also have relied on good teamwork and communication, so there is a lot to think about.

Revision Activity

Completed

Complete the following risk assessment form for the party.

Table 3.4.1

Hazard	Who might be affected	Is risk adequately controlled	Further action taken to control risk
Special dietary requirements	Customers		Clearly identify likely problem dishes on menu Brief staff thoroughly before event
Fire		Fire procedures checked Fire notices checked Fire exits clear	
Hazards relating to food preparation and cooking, e.g. cuts, burns			First-aid kit and trained first aider available Staff fully briefed before event
Accidental trips and falls		Tables set out clearly with paths between Nothing obstructing floor No trailing wires or tablecloths	

3.5 Costing Menus and Events

 Key Facts

Revised

Selling price has to take into account:

- **actual food costs** (cost of all the ingredients)
- **overheads** (rent, rates, gas, electricity, maintenance of equipment)
- **labour costs** (staff wages)
- **profit**
- **VAT** (Value Added Tax).

The **formula used** in the industry is:

$$\frac{\text{Cost per portion} \times 100}{40}$$

Check your understanding

Tested

1   A hotel has calculated the actual cost of one portion of chicken chasseur at £2.86. List three other costs to be considered when calculating the selling price.

2   Calculate the selling price of one portion of chicken chasseur.

Exam tips

Questions on costing often relate to the factors that need to be taken into consideration when calculating selling price and link closely to portion control.

You need to know why portion control is so important, ways of achieving accurate portion control and equipment used for portion control when serving food.

Revision Activity

Completed

Match the following foods to an appropriate method of portion control:

Ladle	Fresh fruit salad
Individual dish	Cheesecake
Ice-cream scoop	Tomato soup
Cutting lines	Creamed potatoes
Sundae dish	Individual lasagne portion

NOTE: There is another activity in Chapter 1.11 on portion control and costing.

3.6 Customer Care and Corporate Image

Key Facts
Revised

Customer care means:

- recognising **customers' needs**
- maintaining customers' **comfort and security**
- making sure customers are **satisfied**.

To achieve good **customer care**, staff need to:

- put customers first
- provide safe, secure, comfortable and hygienic surroundings
- make customers feel valued so that they want to return
- deal promptly and effectively with customer complaints.

Measuring **customer satisfaction** helps organisations provide more effective customer care. Feedback can be verbal, written or informal (observed). The most common methods of measuring customer satisfaction are by:

- comment cards
- questionnaires
- focus groups
- talking to customers
- observing customers
- using mystery customers
- using staff feedback.

Corporate image

Many companies have their own corporate image so they are easily identifiable. Corporate image can be by:

- logo
- uniform
- menu
- layout and décor of the establishment
- advertising.

We value your comments:

The food was ?

The service was ?

Problems were dealt with?

My overall experience was ?

Exam tip

Customer care is extremely important. A hotel may have fantastic food and beautiful surroundings but if the customer care is poor the guests will not return!

Make sure you know how to achieve good customer care (from running your event), how to recognise good customer care, how to measure customer care and the implications of poor customer care.

Check your understanding

1 Explain the importance of good customer care to customers, staff and the owners of a large hotel.

2 Suggest why large chains, e.g. Hilton Hotels, have a corporate image.

Revision Activity

Prepare a chart like the one below showing the implications of good and poor customer care on customers, staff and an establishment.

Table 3.6.1

	Good Customer Care	Poor Customer Care
Customers	Happy customers Returning customers Recommend friends	Unhappy customers Non-returning customers Tell friends about poor service
Staff	High self-esteem Good teamwork Effective communication Loyal to workplace Possible promotion	Low self-esteem Poor teamwork Lack of communication High staff turnover No chance of promotion
Establishment	Profitable Good reputation Low turnover of staff	Likely to go out of business Poor reputation High staff turnover

3.7 Standards of Service

 Key Facts

- Every hospitality establishment will set out its **own standards of service**.
- **Staff training** is the key to achieving and maintaining high standards of service.
- Customers base their expectations on the **level** of service they receive, not on the **type** of service.
- The **level** of service should be attentive, efficient, friendly, welcoming and helpful.
- **Standards of service** are judged on body language, attitude, appearance, manner and tone of voice of staff.
- **All staff should be trained** to meet, greet and say farewell to guests, **respond to enquiries and deal with complaints**.

Complaints procedure

- Listen carefully to the customer – do not interrupt.
- Be sympathetic and show you understand the problem.
- Apologise.
- Tell the customer what you intend to do.
- Act immediately – pass on the information to your supervisor or manager.
- Tell the customer how the problem is being dealt with.
- Apologise again and thank the customer for his or her comments.

Check your understanding

1 A guest complains that the cheesecake served at dinner is still frozen in the middle. Suggest how the wait staff would deal with this problem.

2 A guest rings reception to say that the heating is not working in their hotel room. Suggest how the receptionist would deal with this situation.

Exam tip

Remember it is not the **style** of service but the **level** of service that is important. Customers expect different standards in different establishments. You would not expect the same **standard** of service in a McDonald's as in a five-star hotel – but you would expect the staff to be polite, friendly, welcoming and helpful in both establishments.

Revision Activity

Look at the following picture and explain the improvements you would make if you were the restaurant manager.

3.8 Quality Assurance and 3.9 Quality Control

te

Key Facts

- The quality of a **meal** in a restaurant is easy to assess because it relies on the food being beautifully cooked, attractively presented and having an excellent flavour.
- The quality of **service** depends on the staff giving the service. Staff members need to be reliable, courteous, tactful, smart, polite and friendly.
- The quality of **surroundings** depends upon the facilities, cleanliness, décor, atmosphere, menu offered and prices.

Accommodation

- Star ratings denote the quality of guest accommodation and services including hotels, guest houses, inns, farmhouses and bed and breakfast establishments.

Restaurants

- Michelin stars are awarded to 'exceptional' restaurants.
- AA Rosettes are awarded to the best restaurants serving food with 'care, understanding and skill'.

Check your understanding
Tested

1 Explain why a couple who are looking for a venue to celebrate their 25th wedding anniversary may look at the star ratings of hotels before making a choice.

2 Describe the differences between a guest house and a hotel.

Exam tip

Questions on quality often link to standards of service and customer care, so these topics should be revised together.

Revision Activity
Completed

Prepare a chart like the one below giving as many quality points as you can for each section.
A few examples have been done for you.

Table 3.8.1

	Signs of quality
Food	Beautifully presented Excellent flavour
Accommodation	Spotlessly clean Luxurious furnishings
Service	Staff immaculately dressed Staff make customers feel 'special'

3.10 Teamwork and Communication

 Key Facts ———————————————————— Revised

How to recognise good teamwork:

- Team members work quickly.
- Team members are happy.
- Team members have high self-esteem.
- Team members talk to each other effectively.
- Team members feel able to suggest ideas.
- Team members know what is expected of them.
- Team members accept responsibility.
- Tasks are carried out effectively.

Good team leaders:

- delegate tasks effectively
- supervise their teams
- motivate their teams
- communicate effectively
- give advice, praise and support
- give positive feedback
- maintain quality.

Communication

It is important to communicate effectively in hospitality establishments.

The **accuracy** of communication is particularly important in the following areas:

- administration, for example when dealing with telephone calls, enquiries, reservations, registration and guest accounting
- customer billing, for example when guests pay their account
- booking systems: bookings are the first contact a guest will have with an establishment so it is important to be accurate and create the right impression
- ICT skills, for example good literacy skills when compiling guest databases, word processing and sending emails
- storage of personal data, for example front office staff must be aware of their limitations under the Data Protection Act because they are responsible for guests' security.

The **effectiveness** of communication is particularly important in customer care, for example meeting and greeting guests, checking in and checking out, dealing with enquiries and complaints.

Tested

Check your understanding

1 Discuss the importance of good teamwork when running a hospitality event.

2 Discuss the importance of effective communication between the front office and housekeeping departments of a large hotel.

Exam tip

Questions often relate to how you recognise good teamwork, the importance of teamwork and the importance of effective communication. Learn this section thoroughly.

 ## Revision Activity

Completed

Prepare a chart like the one below showing the implications of good and poor teamwork on customers, staff and an establishment. Note how closely this links to the chart on page 66 on customer care.

Table 3.10.1

	Good teamwork	Poor teamwork
Customers	Happy customers Returning customers Recommend friends	Unhappy customers Non-returning customers Tell friends about poor service
Staff	High self-esteem Happy atmosphere Effective communication Tasks completed quickly Team members accept responsibility Loyal to workplace	Low self-esteem Blame culture may exist Lack of communication Tasks may be incomplete Team members do not accept responsibility High staff turnover
Establishment	Runs smoothly Good reputation Low turnover of staff Profitable	Likely to receive complaints Poor reputation High staff turnover Likely to go out of business

Activity 2

In order to make an event run smoothly, teamwork has to be perfect. Think of a word that starts with each letter of the word perfect in order to help you remember! The following ones are suggestions only – can you think of different ones?

P – polite
E – efficient
R – resourceful
F – friendly
E – enthusiastic
C – courteous
T – tactful

3.11 Environmental Issues

Reduce, reuse and recycle

- Fit large refillable soaps and shower gels in hotel bathrooms.
- Cut down the number of 'give-aways', e.g. sewing kits and shoe cleaning kits supplied in guest bedrooms.
- Ensure that staff recycle glass, tins, card and paper.
- Encourage guests to recycle by supplying bins.
- Do not print out unnecessarily. Pass on information by email.
- Do not put out new toilet rolls for new guests. Fold edges of remaining roll into a peak for neat presentation.
- Buy fresh ingredients that have little or no packaging.
- Reuse large containers for storage.
- Use vegetable peelings for compost.
- Send food waste to local farms to be used as animal food.

Legislation covers the disposal of food and catering waste.

- Some food waste is collected by registered companies which process it into a nutrient-rich fertiliser used for growing crops.
- Other food waste goes to landfill for disposal or is sent to an approved composting or biogas facility.

Conserving energy and water

- Use towels more than once, if guests are happy to do so.
- Fit showers rather than baths.
- Have 'push' taps that send out short bursts of water or automatic taps that sense when hands are underneath.
- Have lights, heating and electrical equipment that work only when a key card is placed in the slot.
- Have air conditioning on only when the guest is in the room.
- Use energy saving light bulbs.
- Set the temperature of hot water and heating.
- Install modern toilets that use less flush water or use grey water for flushing.
- Install energy efficient kettles, hairdryers, etc.
- Turn off TV sets rather than leave on 'standby'.

> At Anglia World Hotels, we know that many of our customers are concerned about protecting the environment. To reduce the amount of water and detergent that we use, we will not remove all towels for cleaning every day during your stay. If you would like your towels to be replaced today, please leave them in the bath.

Check your understanding ──────────────────────── Tested

1 Discuss the ways in which hotels can encourage their customers to conserve energy.

Exam tip

Refer to Chapter 1.14 for exam tips and activities.

4.2 Hospitality Event

Tips for the event

The 'Event' folder should be presented in a logical order. You should ensure that all the linking paragraphs are included so that anyone reading the folder does not have to ask why, what, where or when at the end of any section.

Research checklist

- Thought shower of possible events.
- What the event will be, with reasons. Include any other relevant information (if known at this stage) such as date, time, type of event, number of guests and other team members.
- Where the event will take place, with reasons.
- Notes on teamwork and their importance appropriate to event.
- Notes on nutrition and menu planning appropriate to event.
- Questionnaire, analysis of results and conclusion (if appropriate).
- Notes on types of menu and type chosen for event.
- A list and description of job roles needed for the event.
- A plan of action for the event.
- Notes on type of food service and method chosen for event.

Planning checklist

- Recipes trialled with photographs and evaluation of suitability.
- Final menu chosen with reasons.
- Risk assessment of venue, menu, etc. to include safety, hygiene, HACCP and fire safety.
- Promotional material, e.g. posters, flyers, invitations, menus.
- Methods of portion control, garnishing and decorating (coloured diagrams of how food will be plated are a good idea).
- Shopping list with quantities and prices.
- Time plans for day – one individual plan, one group plan.
- Room plan for kitchen showing where dishes are to be made, cooked and served to avoid cross-contamination.
- Room plan of restaurant.
- Table plan for food service including colour schemes.
- Preparation of waiters' pads.
- Notes on customer care and customer satisfaction.
- Preparation of evaluation forms if using.

Carrying out the event

- Write-up of the event.
- Photographic evidence (of personal appearance, food preparation, food presentation, restaurant layout, food service, customers).

Evaluation

- Comment on individual work – were you able to show a range of skills, safe working practices, hygienic working practices, good teamwork and good customer care? Remember to give valid examples.
- Comment on group work – did your group work well together, did you communicate effectively, were your customers satisfied? Remember to give valid examples.

- Strengths and weaknesses – try to think of at least three strengths and three weaknesses of your work within the event.
- Improvements – explain how you could improve your weaknesses if given the same event again or a similar event in the future.
- Overall event – did the group keep to the budget set, did the event make a profit, was the customer feedback positive, were there any thank you letters, emails, articles in the local paper or school magazine? Remember to include copies of documents such as emails and articles in your folder as evidence.

Here is a thought shower you can use to check you have included all the information you need in your 'Event' folder.

Research – your work should include:
- Thought shower of possible events.
- The event you will carry out with reasons and details of date, time, type of event, number of guests and names of other team members.
- Where event will be – with reasons.
- Notes on teamwork, relevant nutrition, special dietary needs and menu planning.
- Questionnaire, analysis of results and conclusion (if used).
- Menu chosen, with reasons.

Planning – your work should include:
- Recipes trialled with evaluation of suitability.
- Final menu chosen with reasons.
- Promotional material, e.g. posters, flyers.
- Shopping lists.
- Details of portion control, drawings of final garnishing and decorating.
- Time plans for event (group and individual).
- Room plans (kitchen and restaurant).
- Table plans.
- Sample waiters' pads.
- Notes on customer care and customer satisfaction.
- Evaluation cards.

Event

Evaluation – your work should include:
- Comments on individual work – personal appearance and standard of work, teamwork, food preparation, food service and customer care.
- Comments on group work – teamwork, communication, customer satisfaction.
- Comments on strengths and weaknesses of your own and group work. Specific improvements you would make given the task again. Include customer feedback, thank you letters, emails, newspaper articles, etc.

Carrying out event – you will be assessed on:
- Personal hygiene (wearing of whites, hair tied back, etc.).
- Hygienic and safe food preparation.
- Organisation and timing, independent working, confidence and competence.
- Standard of food presentation. Portion control
- Restaurant presentation, food service.
- Customer care and standards of service.
- Handling queries, problems and complaints.

Answers to questions in each topic section

1.1 The Catering Industry

1 Examples of commercial catering establishments include hotels, restaurants, cafeterias, guest houses, public houses and wine bars.

2 Examples of non-commercial catering establishments include hospitals, residential homes, prisons and the armed services.

3 Examples of residential catering establishments include hotels, guest houses, farmhouses, bed and breakfast establishments and public houses.

4 Examples of non-residential catering establishments include schools (school meals), burger vans, restaurants, cafeterias, wine bars and fast-food outlets.

5 Examples of organisations that would employ contract caterers include hospitals, schools, businesses and the armed forces.

6 Advantages of employing a contract caterer for a large garden party are: the contract caterer will organise their own staff to do the making of the food, the layout, the serving and the clearing up, leaving the host/hostess free to enjoy the party.

1.2 Food Service

1 Vending machines are likely to be found at railway stations because they can be used at any time of the day or night (without the need for employing staff), they can be used to dispense a variety of items including food, drink, cigarettes, etc.

2 Advantages of vending machines are: they are clean, hygienic, convenient (available 24 hours a day), offer single portion sizes, take up little space, save employment costs and are generally easy to replenish.

3 Advantages of changing from waited service to buffet service are:
- fewer staff needed, therefore more profit and fewer wages
- customers serve themselves, therefore likely to be less waste and fewer complaints
- kitchen staff do not have to cook individual orders – can bulk cook and put on display
- customers choose their own food from display – do not have to wait to be served
- customers can eat at their own pace and go back for more if they wish.

4 Fast food is popular because the food is of a consistent quality and considered to be good value for money. A limited menu is offered but all food on the menu is always available. Service is quick and food can usually be eaten in or taken away. Some fast-food restaurants offer a drive-through service. They are open long hours and situated in popular shopping centres and high streets. They advertise nationally.

5 Staff serving in a fast-food restaurant should be quick, be able to communicate effectively with customers and other staff members, be clean and hygienic in appearance, be polite and friendly, be good at maths (when working on the tills) and be able to 'up-sell' (encourage customers to have large drinks instead of regular ones, have a dessert and other extras).

6 Staff serving in a five-star hotel must have a very high standard of personal presentation, be formal, attentive and polite, be able to communicate effectively with customers and other members of staff, be able to transfer food from serving dishes to customers' plates quickly and provide a very high level of customer care.

7 A restaurant manager is responsible for organising staff rotas, training and supervising staff, maintaining standards, liaising with front office and kitchen staff, allocating wait staff to tables, dealing with compliments and complaints and in some cases is involved in hiring and firing staff.

1.3 Job Roles, Employment and Training

1 Qualities would be: pleasant and friendly because customers are likely to return, quick to serve so that customers are not kept waiting, to be fit, as they spend a long time on their feet, reliable so that they turn up for work when asked, and honest because they are dealing with money.

2 A 'sous chef' or second chef is the person who is directly in charge of food production and supervision of kitchen staff. This is because the executive chef spends a lot of time in the office purchasing, costing, planning work schedules and planning menus.

3 Casual or seasonal staff are employed at busy times of year and for special functions, e.g. Christmas and New Year, summer season (especially in seaside resorts) and for wedding receptions and dinner dances.

4 Casual staff are often employed through an agency. They do not have a contract or set hours to work. Part-time staff have contracts and work for the same establishment on a permanent basis, although they do fewer hours than full-time staff. They often work the same days every week. Casual staff work at busy times of year or when there are special functions only.

1.4 Health, Safety and Hygiene

1 Food poisoning bacteria include Campylobacter, Salmonella (the most common), E. Coli, Clostridium Perfringens, Listeria, Bacillus Cereus and Staphylococcus Aureus.

2 Symptoms of food poisoning are: nausea (feeling sick), sickness, diarrhoea, stomach ache, fever (high temperature).

3 Chefs wear a hat to prevent hair and dandruff falling into food, to act like a chimney and keep the head cool and in some kitchens to show superiority (the taller the hat, the more important the chef).

4 Personal hygiene rules relate to 'the person' and how they can prevent food poisoning – wearing of clean whites, wearing a hat, having short, clean nails, frequent hand washing (e.g. before preparing food, after visiting the toilet, after handling raw food), covering cuts with a clean blue plaster, not coughing or sneezing over food, etc.

5 Food hygiene rules relate to all 'food handling' – wash fruit and vegetables before use, keep raw and cooked food apart, store raw food below cooked food in a refrigerator, keep food cold, clean and covered, keep food out of the danger zone (5°C to 63°C), use colour-coded chopping boards to prevent cross-contamination, defrost food thoroughly before cooking, check 'use by' dates, etc.

6 Kitchen hygiene rules relate to the cleanliness and organisation of the kitchen – ensure fridges and freezers are at correct temperatures, use food in rotation (FIFO – first in first out), clean as you go, mop up spills immediately, have good cleaning schedules, get rid of waste effectively, have good pest control, etc.

7 First-aid treatment for a burn – immediately place under cold running water and leave for at least 10 minutes or until burning sensation stops. Do NOT apply cream or lotion. For larger burns seek medical advice.

8 Blue detectable plasters are used in catering because they can be seen clearly (as no food is bright blue) and because they have a thin metallic strip in them that would set off an alarm in a factory production line.

9 The temperature of **i.** a refrigerator is 1 °C–5 °C (under 5°C); **ii.** The temperature of a freezer is −18°C (commercially as low as −26 °C); **iii.** The temperature of hot-held food is 63°C.

1.5 Legislation

1 An EHO can enter food premises at any time, inspect food, take away samples of food to be analysed, confiscate any food they think is unfit, issue 'improvement notices' and close down premises.

2 The main aim of the HASAWA is to prevent accidents.

3 HACCP stands for Hazard Analysis Critical Control Points.

4 A risk assessment is a summary of what could cause harm to people in your workplace.

5 In the event of a fire – raise the alarm, call the fire brigade, turn off gas supply, electricity and fans if possible, close windows and doors, try to fight the fire if small enough with appropriate extinguisher or fire blanket but do not put yourself in danger, leave the building and go to the assembly point and do not re-enter the building until directed to do so.

6 Wash your hands; Beware of wet floor.

1.6 Food Preparation

1

Cake-making method	Typical cake made by this method
Creaming method	Victoria sandwich, fairy cakes, rich fruit cake
Whisking method	Swiss roll, sponge
Rubbing-in method	Rock cakes, raspberry buns
Melting method	Gingerbread

2 Possible causes: there may not be enough raising agent – many scones recipes use self-raising (SR) flour and extra baking powder, the dough may have been over-handled or rolled too thinly and the oven may have been too cool. Scones need a very hot, pre-heated oven.

3 Rules for shortcrust pastry making include: keep everything as cool as possible, sieve flour to aerate it before use, use fat straight from the fridge, rub in with fingertips as they are the coolest part of the hands, rub in until the mixture looks like breadcrumbs and is a sandy texture, add cold water, mix with a palette knife, handle dough as little as possible, knead lightly, roll out on a lightly floured table top, do not turn pastry over.

4 Convenience foods are popular with caterers because: they save time, they are of a consistent standard, size and quality, seasonal foods are available all year, they last longer (have later 'use by' or 'best before' dates than fresh food), they produce less waste, there is less risk of cross-contamination because high-risk or raw food is not being used and they are a useful stand-by in case of extra guests, failed deliveries or other emergencies.

5 Rice and pasta can be made more interesting by adding sauces, e.g. Bolognese sauce with spaghetti and curry sauce served with rice. Different varieties of rice and pasta are available which add interest, e.g. brown or wild rice instead of white rice and different pasta shapes, e.g. ravioli, fusilli, spirals. Rice and pasta both make excellent salads. Because they are bland they absorb the flavours of other foods very well and can be used to make delicious dishes such as paella, risotto, biryani. Rice and pasta can both be served in desserts, e.g. rice pudding, pear Condé, sweet ravioli, chocolate fettuccine and dessert lasagne. Although rice and pasta tend to be boiled or steamed, they can be fried, e.g. egg fried rice, or baked, e.g. lasagne.

1.7 Cooking Methods

1 Rules to follow when deep-fat frying include: use a good-quality oil, never fill deep-fat fryer above 'load line', usually about three-quarters full, dry foods thoroughly before frying to prevent spitting, do not fry too much food at once, allow the fat to recover its heat before adding more food and have frying basket, spider and lid to hand for safety reasons.

2 Reasons for the popularity of:
- Grilling – it is considered 'healthier' than frying because the fat from food is allowed to drip off; no fat is needed for cooking; it is a quick method of cooking.
- Stir-frying – a minimum amount of oil is used, therefore it is considered a 'healthy' method of cooking. Food is cooked very quickly (but preparation takes longer).
- Barbecuing – popular for outdoor cooking, especially in the summer; adds a smoky flavour to food.
- A healthy method of cooking as no extra fat is added to food.
- Deep-fat frying – adds colour and flavour to food. Not healthy because food is submerged in fat. One of the most popular cooking methods in the UK.
- Microwaving – cooks and reheats food very quickly (in small quantities). Food can be cooked without adding extra fat or water. Some microwaves do not 'brown' food but special browning dishes can be used.

3 Cuts of beef suitable for grilling are primarily steaks, e.g. minute steak, sirloin steak, rump steak, T-bone steak, fillet steak.

4 Delicate food can be protected when frying by coating in egg and breadcrumbs, flour, batter or pastry.

1.8 Culinary Terms and Presenting Food

1 A high standard of hygiene can be maintained by: ensuring food is kept refrigerated and covered until service, keeping 'extra' supplies refrigerated until required, having separate serving equipment for each dish of food, never topping up high-risk foods like mayonnaise, using tongs, gloves, etc. instead of bare hands to transfer food from one tray to another, wiping down frequently, ensuring good temperature control.

2 Colour is particularly important because 'we eat with our eyes' before tasting the food – if food looks good we want to eat it. If the food itself lacks colour it can be added with careful decoration or garnish, e.g. parsley and tomato on a dish of lasagne or cottage pie. Avoid the use of too much cream, brown or green as they are 'dead' colours and make food appear flat and uninteresting. The colour of serving dishes, lighting and table tops is also important and can add or detract from the appearance of food.

3 Portion control is particularly important for a self-serve buffet where you may want to limit certain items. In many establishments staff members serve the expensive (protein) foods and leave guests to serve themselves with less expensive accompaniments like salads and breads. Portion control can be achieved by the use of cutting lines on items such as quiches and pies, careful garnish, slicing meat, having set numbers of items such as chicken drumsticks and sausage rolls and using specific sized spoons and ladles. Some establishments display notices stating portion size.

1.9 Nutrition and Healthy Eating

1 Nutrients found in cheese include protein, fat, calcium and Vitamins A and D.

2 Fibre is needed by the body to keep the digestive system in good working order. Fibre 'passes through' the body collecting all the waste as it goes until it is 'expelled' from the body. Lack of fibre can lead to constipation.

3 Foods rich in Vitamin C (citrus fruits, kiwi fruit, strawberries, etc.) should be eaten with foods containing iron because Vitamin C helps the body to 'absorb' the iron. (Think about taking a basket of fruit to a patient in hospital. People may be in hospital for an operation or as a result of an accident. Both of these involve a loss of blood: the fruit will supply Vitamin C which in turn helps the body to absorb iron which is needed for red blood cells.)

4 Calcium and Vitamin D are needed for healthy bones and teeth.

5 A vegan does not eat animal flesh or animal products. A lactose intolerant person does not eat milk or milk products. A person with anaemia lacks iron. A diabetic should avoid sugary foods.

1.10 Menu Planning

1 The four Ws are Who (is the menu for), What (type of food is going to be eaten), Where (is it going to be eaten) and When (is it going to be eaten).

2 It is important to have a range of colours and textures in a meal to add interest and appeal. Colour will make the meal look appetising and a range of textures will add to the 'mouth feel' by including crisp, crunchy, smooth, etc.

3 It is important to consider different dietary needs when planning meals because we live in a multicultural society and a hotel will want to attract as many customers as it can. Special diets include vegetarian diets, religious diets and medical diets.

4 A healthy two-course meal for a toddler should contain fruit and vegetables and home-made produce, as far as possible. Examples of suitable main courses include chicken strips (made from chicken breast) served with potato wedges, peas and sweetcorn, home-made meat balls in a tomato sauce served with pasta and home-made fish fingers served with potato wedges, peas and sweetcorn. Suitable desserts include fruit in jelly served with ice cream, yogurt and fresh fruit dippers and simple chocolate pudding served with ice cream.

5 It is important for teenagers to remember that they are still growing – so they should not try to diet (unless they are very overweight and have sought medical advice). Healthy eating should be simple – not complicated. Breakfast is a must and is needed to 'kick start' the body's metabolism (the rate at which it burns up calories) in the morning and to provide energy to last till break or lunch time. Eat as many fruits and vegetables as possible – an apple for break, a ham or cheese and salad sandwich for lunch, fruit juices or water rather than fizzy drinks and a good meal in the evening. Take-away meals are fine in moderation but if used, try to choose healthier options like thin-crust pizzas, wedges rather than chips, boiled rice instead of fried rice, no heavy sauces, etc.

1.11 Portion Control and Costing

1 If a chicken dish costs £2.40 to make, the selling price would be calculated using the formula below:

$$\frac{2.40 \times 100}{40}$$

The answer is £6.00.

2 Portion control can be achieved by: using cutting lines, careful garnish or decoration, using individual dishes, using standard sized equipment like ladles and spoons, using specific weights of food like a 100g fish fillet and using standard recipes.

3 The advantages of portion control are: customer satisfaction (a fair portion for a fair price, having the same size portion as other customers), prevention of waste, makes ordering easier, makes costing easier, makes profit.

1.12 Specialist Equipment

1 Cook's knife; ladle; potato masher.

2 Choose a set of knives made of stainless steel because they will not rust, are easy to sharpen (or if expense is not a problem, the kind that will never need sharpening), are of good quality, are the right weight to hold comfortably, have good handles that are comfortable to hold (plastic are the most common) and contain the most useful sizes.

3 The essential knives are:
- cook's knife, used for chopping, cutting, slicing and shredding
- vegetable or paring knife, used for chopping, cutting and slicing small items of food
- peeler, used for peeling fruit and vegetables
- palette knife, used for lifting, scraping, turning and spreading.

4 The rules to follow when using knives include: use a knife of an appropriate size for the food to be cut, carry point down by the side of your body, pass by the handle only, keep handle clean, dry and grease-free, keep knives sharp,

never place in a bowl or sink of washing-up water, store knives carefully in a block or drawer, keep fingers tucked in (bridge grip) when chopping.

5 Fridges and freezers need to work efficiently in order to keep food at the correct temperatures (1 °C–5 °C for fridges and at least −18 °C for freezers). If food is not stored at the correct temperature it will 'go off' quickly and may pose a health risk to customers.

6 A microwave can be used for defrosting, reheating and cooking food. Some commercial ovens combine convection and microwave energy and when used together speed up the cooking time and give food a good colour and texture. A fast-food outlet concentrates on savoury food. Microwave ovens tend to be used to quickly reheat desserts.

1.13 Communication and Record-keeping

1 A storekeeper needs to keep accurate records so that they have supplies at the right time and in the correct quantities. It helps prevent waste, reduces risk of theft, ensures stock is in good condition when needed as it is used in rotation, e.g. oldest first or first in first out (FIFO), and ensures accurate food costing.

2 The types of communication would be:
- restaurant booking – telephone call
- placing a food order to a regular supplier – email, fax or telephone call
- finding out about a holiday hotel – internet.

3 An accident form would record: the name, age and sex of the injured person, their job title, their address, the date and time of the accident, the nature (type) of the accident, the nature (type) of the injury, the action taken (first aid and any other treatment) and witness details.

4 ICT is important to the catering industry because it can be used for communication, record-keeping and planning. Specific uses include reservation systems, management systems, stock control systems, events management, menu engineering and dietary analysis.

1.14 Environmental Issues

1 Catering establishments are encouraged to take a lead in environmental issues. This is to keep within the law, control costs, conserve raw materials and energy and improve efficiency. Many customers favour establishments with environmental policies.

2 Tips for saving energy in a restaurant include ensuring temperature is kept at a level that is comfortable for customers and staff. If a restaurant is too hot it wastes energy, too cool and customers will not return. Use dispensers for salt, sugar, sauces, etc. to avoid waste.

3 'Biodegradable' means it will decompose, break down, compost or degrade by natural means. 'Recyclable' means it can be re-processed to be used again, made into something else, used again.

1.15 Food Packaging

1
Polystyrene box	Burger
Flat, cardboard box	Pizza
Foil container with card lid	Chicken biryani
Clear triangular plastic box	BLT sandwich
Cardboard cone	French fries
Plastic container with lid	Sweet and sour pork

3.1 The Hospitality Industry

1 Establishments found in the entertainment and leisure sector of the industry include: spa centres, leisure centres, golf clubs, sporting venues, e.g. race tracks and football clubs, bowling alleys, cinemas, theatres, etc.

2 A hotel may employ a mixture of permanent, part-time and casual staff because each one offers something different. Full-time staff are employed on a permanent basis and often work set shifts over a seven-day period, including weekends. Part-time staff 'cover' for full-time staff on their days off and holidays and are often employed for the busiest times of the week, e.g. weekends, mealtimes (kitchen or restaurant) and checking-out times in the morning (front office). Casual staff work for specific functions, e.g. wedding parties, dinner dances and at busy times of year, e.g. Christmas, Easter, summer in seaside resorts.

3.2 Types of Service and Client Groups

1 Think of the four main areas as discussed in the Key facts – accommodation, food and drink, meeting room, facilities and equipment.
  - Accommodation: car parking, area for coats and toilet facilities.
  - Food and drink: fridge space for food storage, tea and coffee making facilities, food preparation facilities; type of service required, e.g. tray, table.
  - Meeting room: layout of tables and chairs, layout of serving tables, space for serving food, wheelchair access.
  - Facilities and equipment: table linen, paper napkins, crockery and cutlery, decorations (if special occasion), cleaning equipment to clean hall at end.

2 The delegates are likely to need accommodation the night before if the meeting starts early in the morning and they live some distance away. They will need food and drink throughout the day (breakfast, break, lunch, tea and dinner), water, juice and sweets on tables in the meeting room, and delegate packs (pens, paper, etc.), Any delegates with special needs should be catered for, e.g. wheelchair access and those with special dietary needs.

3.3 Job Roles, Employment and Training

1 A receptionist working in a five-star hotel would need the following qualities: a warm, polite and efficient manner; the ability to make guests feel welcome and important; the ability to solve problems and multi-task; a high standard of literacy and numeracy; should be highly organised with the ability to delegate tasks effectively; the ability to train others and a calm, reassuring manner.

2 A night porter is responsible for checking guests in and out of the hotel at night and also dealing with any queries, problems or complaints.

3 Casual staff are employed at busy times of year, e.g. Christmas, New Year, Easter, Bank Holidays, and for special functions, e.g. dinner dances, wedding receptions.

3.4 Planning for Functions and Events

1 For a golden wedding the room should be decorated accordingly, with gold balloons, streamers and banners on the walls and gold flowers, napkins and table confetti on white or cream table linen. Photographs of the couple on their wedding day, plus perhaps a photograph board showing memorable moments of their 50 years together, could be displayed in the main part of the room. A formal table layout would be the best option to celebrate the anniversary.

The type of food could be either a buffet or sit-down meal. As the couple are older, it would be less stressful for them to have a sit-down meal where the food is served. The guests will include a range of different ages, sexes, likes and dislikes and a sit-down meal would be the easier option. The couple could be asked for their favourite dishes to be served, as long as alternatives are provided for any guests with special dietary needs. If a buffet were to be offered, then a fork buffet would be more appropriate than a finger buffet for a golden wedding, so that guests who have travelled any distance or have to travel home have a more substantial meal.

2 It is important for Stan and Joan to have good communication with the party organiser because:
  - the organiser will know their expectations
  - the organiser will find out about any guests with special dietary needs, favourite foods, favourite music, the budget, etc.
  - Stan and Joan will feel involved in the decision making and will also feel confident the event will be successful
  - the event is likely to go to plan.

3.5 Costing Menus and Events

1 When calculating selling price the following costs have to be taken into account:
  - overheads – gas, electricity, rates, maintenance of equipment, etc.
  - labour costs – staff wages
  - profit
  - VAT (currently 20%).

2 If a portion of chicken chasseur costs £2.86 to make then the selling price would be calculated as:

$$\frac{2.86 \times 100}{40} = 7.15$$

The answer is £7.15.

3.6 Customer Care and Corporate Image

1 Customer care is important for the following reasons:
- Customers – their needs will be met, they are likely to return and they are likely to recommend your hotel to others.
- Staff – they will have high self-esteem, they will be loyal to the hotel and they will be happy in their work.
- Hotel owners – will have increased profit, a stable staff (which saves on recruitment and training costs) and a good reputation (which should lead to more guests).

2 Large companies have a corporate image so that they are immediately recognised by customers who know what to expect of the 'brand'. A corporate image can include the company logo (brand), uniform, the menu, the layout of the establishment and company advertising.

3.7 Standards of Service

1 The wait staff should apologise, tell the customer they are going to deal with the complaint, take the frozen cheesecake back to the kitchen and tell the head chef and also tell the restaurant manager. The restaurant manager would apologise to the customer again, offer an alternative and some form of compensation, e.g. a free drink, and ensure the customer is happy with the outcome.

2 The receptionist should apologise to the customer, contact maintenance straight away and establish whether the guest is happy to stay in the room if the problem can be resolved or wants to change rooms immediately. Offer an upgrade of room if available and some form of compensation, e.g. a bottle of wine, to apologise for the inconvenience.

3.8 and 3.9 Quality Assurance and Quality Control

1 Hotels are classified according to star ratings. A hotel with a one-star rating will offer basic facilities and a five-star hotel will offer a full range of facilities and luxurious surroundings. The star rating of hotels will give a good indication of the facilities the couple can expect to find and the price they will be expected to pay.

2 A guest house will offer: en-suite bedrooms (which may be smaller than hotel rooms), limited facilities, no room service, bed and breakfast only, TV, tea and coffee making facilities in room, set menu for breakfast, no pool, gym or health suite, few staff so a more personal service. It will be reasonably priced. A hotel will offer: a choice of rooms, e.g. single, double, twin, family, suites, en-suite facilities, choice of restaurants, TV, hairdryer, tea and coffee-making facilities in room, bar, health suite, pool, conference facilities, room service, someone on reception 24 hours a day, internet access in rooms, etc.

3.10 Teamwork and Communication

1 Teamwork is important to ensure the event runs smoothly. Staff need to communicate with each other so that they understand their job role, their responsibilities and know what is expected of them. With good teamwork all tasks will be carried out quickly and efficiently, and if the staff appear happy the guests will enjoy themselves.

2 There needs to be effective communication between front office staff and housekeeping staff so that staff know which rooms are occupied, which guests are staying, which guests are leaving, if there are any special requirements, e.g. flowers, fruit or champagne, any VIP guests and any problems with the room that need to be dealt with by maintenance staff.

3.11 Environmental Issues

1 Hotels can encourage customers to conserve energy by:
- placing notices in rooms asking customers to turn off lights and power when the room is unoccupied
- asking customers to turn off TVs and computers rather than leaving them on standby
- not replacing towels every day
- providing showers rather than baths
- encouraging customers to recycle newspapers, card, glass, tins and plastic by having suitably placed recycling bins in the hotel.

Success in the examination

The questions will often need specific knowledge and understanding. Those at the beginning of the examination will test knowledge rather than understanding. The questions towards the end of the examination test knowledge *and* understanding.

You may be asked to:
- **define** (give the meaning of)
- **list** (make a list)
- **state** (write clearly but briefly)
- **describe** (give an account of)
- **discuss** (give important aspects of; give advantages and disadvantages of; give benefits and constraints of)
- **explain** (make something clear, giving your reasons)
- **suggest** (advise or recommend)
- **evaluate** (give important aspects of; give your opinion of)
- **assess** (consider, weigh up, evaluate, make a judgement about).

Some students find it easier to write in 'bullet points'. This can look the same as 'writing a list' so it is important to expand the answers and give facts, reasons and examples and not one-word answers.

In the examination

- Follow the instructions given on the front of the exam paper.
- Read each question carefully and highlight or underline key points.
- Check the number of marks available for each question – remember that questions near the end of the paper are marked according to criteria ('criteria marked'), so you may have to give six or eight points to earn four marks.
- Ensure your answers are relevant.
- Keep an eye on the time.
- Leave time to read through your answers – have you given facts, reasons and examples throughout?

Hospitality and Catering Examinations in detail

Topics common to both examinations

These topics are:
- Health, safety and hygiene (known as risk assessment in Unit 4)
- Food preparation, production and presentation, including portion control and costing
- The industry – job roles, employment and training
- Menu planning, including healthy eating
- Communication
- Environmental considerations.

Health, safety and hygiene

You should know the following laws/legislation and the main health, safety and hygiene points and be able to carry out a risk assessment:

- HACCP – hazard analysis critical control points
- Food Safety Act
- Hygiene Regulations
- Key temperatures
- Food poisoning – types, symptoms and prevention
- HASAWA – Health and Safety at Work Act
- Accident prevention and accident procedures
- First aid
- Fire prevention and fire procedures.

Food preparation, production and presentation, including costing and portion control

Most of this section will be learned through practical work and assessed through catering controlled assessments/hospitality events. You should know the importance of hygiene, good working methods, portion control, accurate costing, attractive presentation of food and how to achieve quality products. This section links to health, safety and hygiene, menu planning, kitchen equipment and environmental issues.

Job roles, employment and training

You should know the qualities and duties of the range of staff employed in the hospitality and catering industry.

Menu planning, including healthy eating

You need a sound knowledge of menu planning. You need to know about dietary guidelines, healthy eating campaigns (Eat for Health, Healthy Schools, five-a-day fruit and vegetable campaign) and dietary related disorders, for example obesity, diabetes and anaemia.

You should be able to plan meals for special groups, including the very young, older people, vegans, vegetarians, ethnic groups, lactose or wheat intolerant people and those with allergies to nuts, seafood, etc. You should be able to discuss what foods these customers can and cannot eat and how these foods can be identified on a menu.

Environmental considerations

You should be able to discuss ways in which the hospitality and catering industry can conserve energy and water and reduce waste.

Topics specific to **Hospitality** and **Catering Unit 2**

Commodities

You need to know how 'useful' a commodity is to a caterer and also consider:

- nutritive value
- use and versatility – the type of dishes it can be used in, e.g. sweet, savoury, can it be eaten raw, cooked, hot, cold, at different meal times
- ease of preparation and cooking

- colour, flavour and texture
- ease of obtaining
- storage
- cost.

Nutrition

You need a sound knowledge of basic nutrition, linked to healthy eating and menu planning. You should be able to discuss the impact of living in a multi-ethnic society.

Specialist equipment

You should have knowledge of the use, care and safety of equipment used in the hospitality and catering industry.

Record-keeping and communication

You need to know the importance of accurate record-keeping and the types of record-keeping used in the industry. You should be able to name the different methods of communicating and explain how effective they are in different situations.

You should know how ICT is used in the industry.

Packaging

You should be able to discuss modern food packaging.

Topics specific to **Hospitality** and **Catering Unit 4**

Planning for functions and events

You should have knowledge of:

- types of functions and events
- appropriate choice of venue, date and time
- menu and type of service
- number of guests
- costing
- promotion and advertising
- décor and presentation
- room layout and table layout
- menu cards/place names
- staffing
- risk assessment.

Customer care and standards of service

You should be aware of standards of customer care, methods of measuring customer care, how to deal with problems and complaints and the importance of presenting a positive image to the customer. You need to understand the importance of corporate image. You need to know about measures of quality assurance and quality control.

Teamwork and communication

You need to know how to recognise good teamwork, the importance of effective teamwork and the importance of effective communication in administrative procedures, booking systems, billing customers, customer care, ICT skills and data protection.

Sample Examination Questions, Model Answers and Mark Schemes

Unit 2 Examination Question

The following examples are case study questions that come at the end of the examination paper. Note how parts (b) and (c) are 'criteria marked' – marks are awarded for showing good knowledge and understanding of the question.

Question 1

Janice has decided to set up a contract catering business. She has been asked to cater for a silver wedding anniversary. The couple have requested a three-course lunch that will be served at their home.

(a) Give **two** benefits of employing a contract caterer for this event. [2]

(b) Explain the importance of effective communication between Janice and the customer [4]

(c) Discuss the main points that Janice would need to consider when:
  (i) **costing** the event
  (ii) **planning** the event. [9]

Student A

(a) good quality food
walks home with a good profit

`0`

(b) Janice needs to be able to speak clearly to the customers. Some of the family may be older people. She needs to be able to understand exactly what the couple want for their meal, what time they want it and how much she should make, etc.

`1`

(c) When costing the event Janice should consider the price of all of the ingredients she is using, all the equipment she is using and how much it may cost her to travel there.
When planning the event Janice should consider decorating the room if necessary and should stick to the colour silver as it's the couple's silver wedding anniversary. She should include a good design of how the food should be set out on the plate. She may need to include seasonings so she should confirm with the couple if they do want it and what type of seasonings. She should have a card out so the customers can see what they are eating. She should also ask if there are any special dietary needs that she needs to be aware of.

`4`

`5`

Rationale (reasons) for marks awarded

a No marks awarded – no knowledge of contract caterers evident.

b 1 mark awarded – the student has stated what should be communicated and not the importance of effective communication. Answer is quite vague.

c 4 marks awarded – this is the bottom of the mid-range mark. The student has acknowledged costs of ingredients and travel, but has not mentioned customer's budget for the event, labour costs or the need to make a profit. In the planning section, colour schemes and special dietary needs are mentioned but the rest is very sketchy.

Total mark awarded 5/15 (borderline E/F grade)

Student B

(a) a contract caterer will organise the party for you [1]

they must include what you want and you can design the menu

(b) The customer could use different methods of communication such as verbal, ICT, email and [4] written. This is important so that Janice understands fully what the customer requires, e.g. any favourite dishes, what decorations are needed and any customers who have special dietary needs. Good communication means good service and customer care. Janice and the customer can work together on planning meals for the customer's needs. Written communication is important so that Janice has a record of what the customer wants to be served.

(c) Costing the event – stick to a budget so that Janice can give the customer a good guide [6] price. Buy fairly cheap ingredients so that the customer does not have to pay a lot. Make sure the price she charges the customer provides her with a profit for the ingredients and her time so that she does not go out of business. Do not charge a ridiculous amount, i.e. try to give the customer good value for money whilst making a profit so that her business gets a good reputation.

Planning the event – ask the customer the foods they would like so that she can buy ingredients and decide on cooking methods. As it's a silver wedding anniversary ask the customer whether they want anything specific, for example silver decorations on cakes. Understand what food the customer requires, know the exact time, date and venue of the event. Take into consideration that the people attending may be vegetarian so include vegetarian dishes. If people from ethnic backgrounds are attending have suitable foods (e.g. Jews abide by Kosher rules).

[11]

Rationale (reasons) for marks awarded

a 1 mark awarded – a contract caterer would be employed to organise the party. The second point is a repeat of the first.

b 4 marks awarded – effective communication will lead to a good understanding of the customer's requirements as well as good service and customer care.

c 6 marks awarded – this is the top of the mid-range mark. Answer shows an understanding of the importance of sticking to a budget, charging for ingredients and time and making a profit. The planning section includes the need for silver decorations, the importance of the exact time, date and venue for the event and an acknowledgement of special dietary needs.

NOTE: The mark scheme specifies that in order to achieve a higher mark (7–9) the answer must show a very good understanding of costing. In this case, the costing section needed more information relating to number of guests and any specific needs, decoration costs, overheads such as gas, electricity and petrol costs and labour/staff costs.

Total mark awarded 11/15 (a B grade)

Actual mark scheme for Question 1

a Award **1 mark** for each **correct** answer   (2)

- A contract caterer will take over responsibility for the planning and organising, leaving the customer free to enjoy the party.
- They may prepare and cook food in advance and deliver to the site or cook it on site.
- They decorate the venue.
- They may provide staff to serve the food.

b Award **1–2 marks** for a basic answer that suggests one or two reasons why communication is important. Answer may resemble a list.

Award **3–4 marks** for a very good discussion on the importance of communication between contract caterer and client.

Award a maximum of 2 marks where a candidate has stated **what** should be communicated instead of **why** there should be effective communication.

The answer could include reference to the following:

- Contract caterer needs to keep in contact throughout planning stage to know expectations and requests of customer.
- Contract caterer finds out about special dietary needs, likes and dislikes, favourite food/music of couple, etc. so planning is smooth.
- Customer feels involved in decision making.
- Customer is able to offer suggestions for decorating venue.
- Customer feels confident that event will be successful.
- Event is likely to go to plan, as everyone is aware of what is happening.
- Shows good customer care – more business and good reputation for Janice, as customers will tell others.

c Award **1–3 marks** for a basic understanding of what is important when costing and planning the lunch. Answer may resemble a list.

Award **4–6 marks** for a good understanding of the important points to consider when costing and planning the lunch.

Award **7–9** marks for an excellent understanding of the important points to consider when costing and planning the lunch. (Marks awarded in this top band must show a very good understanding of costing.)

The answer may include reference to the following points:
Costing the event:

- food costs
- decoration costs
- overheads such as gas, electricity, rates, etc. if cooking off site; also petrol/diesel costs for travel and transporting food to venue
- labour costs (if staff are needed for preparing and/or serving food)
- profit
- some contract caterers offer fixed-price menus – but customers may want event personal to them and choose their own menu.

Planning the event:

- age, sex, occupation, special dietary needs (vegetarians, religious and ethnic needs, allergies and intolerances), likes and dislikes of guests
- the time of year (a lighter meal will be needed in summer)
- the time of day (lunchtime menus are often lighter)
- venue (held in the house or garden?)
- space available – lunch requested so how many can comfortably be catered for?
- facilities available – will the lunch be made on/off site?
- will serving equipment or staff be needed?
- type of menu requested – a three-course lunch for a special occasion (candidate may suggest suitable dishes)
- any special requests for dishes – customer favourites, etc.
- will menu be served at a table or offered buffet style?
- layout of room, tables, etc.
- decoration of tables, room (or garden) where event will be held – needs to match silver theme.

Question 2

Winston owns a contract catering company. He has a booking for a party for 12 guests. The client has requested the following menu:

> Melon with Parma Ham
> *
> Stuffed Chicken Breasts in a Creamy Leek Sauce
> *
> New Potatoes
> *
> Baby Carrots, Mange Tout and Baby Sweetcorn
> *
> Ice Cream Profiteroles with Chocolate Sauce
> *
> Selection of Cheese and Home-made Oat Biscuits
> *
> Coffee and Mints

On the morning of the party, Winston's supplier rings up and says that he is unable to get any baby carrots or mange tout.

(a) Discuss how Winston would deal with this problem. [4]

During the morning, the client rings to say that a guest is lactose intolerant.

(b) Explain the changes Winston would have to make for this guest. [4]

Winston's company is very successful.

(c) Evaluate the factors that contribute to the success of a contract catering company. [10]

Model Answers

Student A

(a) He would call up his customer and say that he is unable to supply them with baby carrots or mange tout, he could then ask her if there is any alternative to the carrots or mange tout.   **1**

(b) He may have to take away the ice cream and coffee for this guest and replace them with an alternative dessert that the two can agree on.   **1**

(c) One aspect would be fulfilling the customers' needs on things such as food.   **3**
But also good texture, colour and taste to the food he produces.
Portion control is key to keeping all his customers happy – this could result in returning customers. Also good hygienic rules such as wash hands and use suitable chopping boards for right equipment.

5

Rationale (reasons) for marks awarded

a 1 mark awarded – for contacting client and explaining problem.

b 1 mark awarded for 'take away the ice cream and coffee for this guest'. No more marks can be awarded because not all dishes containing lactose are identified and no alternatives are suggested.

c 3 marks awarded – answer shows a basic understanding of the factors that contribute to the success of a contract catering company. The factors mentioned include meeting customers' needs, good portion control, attractive food and good hygiene policies.

Total mark awarded 5/18 (an F grade)

Student B

(a) Firstly he would try to find another supplier and see if they are able to provide him with the ingredients needed. If that fails then he would have to ring the client and explain to him what has happened. Winston could also work out a suitable alternative to the missing ingredients, allowing the party to go ahead, possibly large carrots cut into sticks and green beans instead of mange tout.

`3`

(b) He would have to do one stuffed chicken breast without the creamy leek sauce because they would not be able to eat cream. Maybe a tomato sauce or gravy could be served instead. Ice cream contains dairy products, therefore an alternative dessert would have to be arranged, possibly a fresh fruit tartlet. They would also not be allowed to eat ordinary cheese so would either have to miss that course or buy lactose-free cheese. Coffee could be served with soya milk.

`4`

(c) A good reputation often means repeat custom so if he is liked and provides a good service he is likely to be hired again. Any staff he employs need to be friendly, polite and well trained to maintain this reputation.

`9`

Good communication with the client is very important, if this happened then client feels involved more and things run smoothly. Problems need to be sorted straight away.

Good food hygiene is another factor; if food is handled properly and safely it reduces the risk of bacteria, therefore making the food safer to eat and ensuring the guests do not suffer from food poisoning. Food should be stored, prepared and cooked properly to ensure good temperature control (kept out of danger zone of 5°C–63°C).

They need to be reasonably priced; a caterer has to include a lot of things when planning his costs such as overheads, staffing and profit. However to be employed again they can't be too expensive so have to plan their costs well. A high quality of ingredients is important; the client is paying you to provide good food therefore the ingredients must be of a good quality.

They have to be a high skilled caterer; if a client wants something that is a high skilled dish, the caterer must be able to make it. If the caterer can only provide dishes that are low skilled, they won't be hired for many events. Good presentation skills are also important; the dishes have to look good and appealing, the dishes served have to be colourful otherwise customers will not want to eat them. They need to be aware of different religions that can't eat certain foods together or at all. For example Jews have to have kosher meat and meat and dairy products can't be served in the same meal. They also need to know about allergies and special diets. Coeliacs cannot eat wheat therefore can't eat something like bread. Special diets could include people who are vegetarian, which means they can't eat meat, therefore the caterer would have to think of alternative dishes.

`16`

Rationale (reasons) for marks awarded

a 3 marks awarded – find another supplier, contact client and explain problem. Realistic alternatives suggested for the carrots and mange tout.

b 4 marks awarded – unable to have cream, ice cream, cheese and milk. Very good understanding is shown and there are suggested alternatives to the dishes affected.

c 9 marks awarded – marks awarded in top mark band because of excellent understanding shown. A lot of factors identified, including good communication skills, building a good reputation, employing good staff, pricing, including labour costs, overheads and profit, good hygiene standards to prevent food poisoning, quality of ingredients and finished dishes, presentation skills and catering for special dietary needs.

Total mark awarded 16/18 (an A* grade)

a Award 1 mark for each suggestion of how Winston would deal with the problem. Alternatives need to be suggested for full marks.
- Try a different supplier.
- Ask supplier what alternatives are available and contact client to explain problem and ask client to make the decision about the alternatives.
- Apologise to the client, offer a reduction.
- Suggest alternatives, e.g. baby carrots could be changed to baton carrots – the colour remains the same so there is a good colour contrast with vegetables, maybe roasted cherry vine tomatoes could be used as an alternative – strong colour contrast again. Mange tout could be changed to sugar snap peas or dwarf green beans – similar colour, which is the most important factor. Other green vegetables may not go as well with the rest of the main course (broccoli could be an exception).
- Offer a frozen alternative.

b Award 1–2 marks for an answer that shows a little understanding of lactose intolerance and the changes that would have to be made to the menu.

Award 3–4 marks for a detailed answer that shows a very good understanding of lactose intolerance and the changes that would have to be made to the menu.

Lactose intolerance is a reaction to lactose (milk sugar) found in milk, cheese, butter, yoghurt and processed foods containing milk products.

Award 1 mark for some explanation of how to deal with lactose intolerance, e.g. change menu to non-dairy.

Changes needed on the menu:
- Starter causes no problem.
- Main course – chicken breast would have to be plain (stuffing not given, sauce probably made with milk therefore could not eat). Winston could offer a gravy or other sauce, e.g. tomato to go with chicken.
- New potatoes and other vegetables would need to be served without adding butter.
- Dessert – ice cream should not be served; cream should be used to fill profiteroles. Chocolate sauce could not be served.
- Cheese could not be eaten unless Winston could buy lactose-free cheese.
- Soya milk could be used for coffee.

c Award 1–2 marks for an answer that shows a limited understanding of the factors that contribute to the success of a contract catering company.

Award 3–5 marks for an answer that shows a basic understanding of the factors that contribute to the success of a contract catering company.

Award 6–7 marks for an answer that shows a clear understanding of the factors that contribute to the success of a contract catering company.

Award 8–10 marks for an answer that shows an excellent understanding of the factors that contribute to the success of a contract catering company.

Answers could include the following:
- Excellent communication skills – dealing with clients, suppliers and staff.
- Excellent customer care skills – dealing with clients and guests.
- Knowledge of menu planning – planning meals for different clients and situations.
- Knowledge of nutrition, special dietary needs – planning meals for different client groups, adapting recipes when needed.
- Good practical and presentation skills – producing quality dishes.
- Consistent quality and portion control.
- Speed and efficiency – the ability to serve food quickly for a large party so that hot food is served hot and not cold.
- Flexibility and adaptability – the ability to 'think on feet' as every situation is different.
- Good reputation – by pleasing clients, being punctual, trustworthy, etc.
- Safe and hygienic – meeting all legislation regarding HACCP, Hygiene Regulations, Food Safety Act, HASAWA, fire regulations, etc.
- Ability to cost menus and calculate a portion size that is appropriate for clients.
- Ability to calculate selling price that is competitive but profitable.
- Having staff who share the same vision for the company.
- Keeping accurate records.
- Good relationships with suppliers.
- Good choice of equipment for food preparation, storage and transport.
- Able to meet deadlines.
- Good advertising/own website.

Unit 4 Examination Question

John has just started work on reception in a large hotel. He works with other staff and uses a number of different ways of communicating with colleagues and clients. He is keen and enthusiastic and hopes to be promoted within the company.

(a) State two methods of communication he will use on reception and give an example of when each type could be used. [4]

(b) Explain why John and his colleagues need to communicate with the head housekeeper. [4]

(c) Discuss the skills and qualities needed by a hotel receptionist. [6]

(d) Assess the importance of teamwork within the hospitality industry. [6]

Student A

(a) Email
Sending a message to a guest

Telephone
Taking bookings

[4]

(b) John and his colleagues need to communicate with the head housekeeper so that they know what guests are leaving and which rooms need to be cleaned.

[1]

(c) A hotel receptionist needs to be organised because they have to make sure the guests have the right rooms. They need to be smartly dressed and polite because they are the first person a guest sees when they arrive.

[2]

(d) Teamwork is really important so that jobs get done quickly and the guests are happy.

[2]

[9]

Rationale (reasons) for marks awarded

a 4 marks awarded for two correct answers and examples.

b 1 mark awarded for a simple list – only two reasons offered.

c 2 marks awarded – for organised, smartly dressed and polite. Only a basic understanding is shown in the answer.

d 2 marks awarded – for jobs done quickly and guests are happy. Only a basic understanding is shown in the answer.

Total mark awarded 9/20 (a D grade)

Student B

(a) Telephone [4]
Taking bookings and answering queries

Pager
Calling staff

(b) John and his colleagues need to communicate with the head housekeeper so that the housekeeper [4]
knows how many guests are expected and if any guests have special requirements, e.g. a cot in
the room, flowers, fruit or champagne. The housekeeper needs to know which guests are leaving
so that the rooms are prepared for a departure. They also need to know which guests are staying
because the cleaning schedules are different. If the housekeeper knows that rooms are going to be
vacant they could be deep cleaned, decorated or any repairs completed. Guests report problems
to reception so John may need to pass on any problems in the room, so that maintenance can be
called before cleaning takes place. Rooms may need to be ready for early arrivals.

(c) A hotel receptionist is the first person a guest sees and first impressions count. A hotel [6]
receptionist should be extremely well groomed, smart and personable. They should make good
eye contact and greet all guests with a smile. They need good communication skills and be able to
speak more than one language, especially in large cities and tourist areas. A receptionist needs
to be very organised, so that accurate records are kept, patient and diplomatic, especially with
difficult guests. They need an excellent knowledge of the hotel and the local area. They need
to have good literacy and ICT skills as much of their work involves processing data and keeping
accurate records. A hotel receptionist has to deal with phone calls, guests and staff so needs
to be able to do several jobs at once.

(d) Teamwork is extremely important in the hospitality industry. Good teamwork means that jobs [6]
get done quickly and usually with fewer problems. If teamwork is good, staff help each other
and this leads to greater self-esteem. If teamwork is good, staff appear happy in their work,
customers get served more quickly and this is seen as good customer care. Good teamwork
means staff communicate well with one another so that information is passed on quickly.
Good teamwork makes tasks easier for staff and work appears effortless to customers.

[20]

Rationale (reasons) for marks awarded

a 4 marks awarded for two correct answers and examples.

b 4 marks awarded for an excellent answer that covers all points on the mark scheme.

c 6 marks awarded for an excellent answer that details the skills and qualities needed by a hotel receptionist.
Examples are given to emphasise main points.

d 6 marks awarded for an excellent answer that shows a detailed understanding of teamwork.

Total mark awarded 20/20 (an A* grade)

Actual mark scheme for Hospitality question

a Award 1 mark for each correct answer and 1 mark for each correct example:
- fax – relaying bookings
- telephone – taking bookings
- email – taking booking, confirming booking
- paper – passing on information
- text – passing on information
- talking – discussing issues
- memo – passing on information
- pager – calling staff
- ICT – relaying messages, accounting
- noticeboard – passing on information, details of local events
- posters – advertising tourist information
- Braille/sign language – communicating with blind, deaf.

b Award 1 mark for a simple list of suggestions with little explanation.

Award 2–3 marks for an answer that includes a range of points with some discussion.

Award 4 marks for a comprehensive answer with a wide range of points and good discussion.

Answers could include:
- to know how many guests are expected
- so that reception staff know which rooms are ready (before giving keys to guests)
- repairs are reported and completed
- so that both departments are aware of any problems
- housekeeper knows which rooms are for departures/stays so that rooms can be prepared accordingly
- any special requirements are ready for guests (flowers, fruit, etc.).

c Award 1–2 marks for an answer that demonstrates only a basic knowledge of the role of a receptionist. The answer may resemble a list.

Award 3–4 marks for an answer that demonstrates good knowledge of the role of a receptionist. The answer will include some discussion.

Award 5–6 marks for a detailed answer that demonstrates a sound knowledge of the role of a receptionist. The answer will contain detailed discussion.

Answers could include:
- clean and well presented to create a good 'first impression'

- good communication skills – the ability to communicate with people of all ages
- ability to speak more than one language – especially in tourist areas and large cities
- able to multi-task – a receptionist often has to deal with guests, members of staff and answer the telephone – all at the same time
- good ICT and literacy skills – for letter writing, preparing bills, etc.
- courteous and friendly at all times
- patient, especially with difficult guests, and able to cope under pressure
- knowledge of the local area – to suggest tourist destinations, locality of shops, buses, trains, taxis, etc. to guests
- be flexible in working hours – to fit in with demands of establishment
- the ability to work as a member of a team – teamwork is essential in making an establishment run smoothly.

d Award 1–2 marks for an answer that demonstrates only a basic knowledge of teamwork. The answer may resemble a list.

Award 3–4 marks for an answer that demonstrates good knowledge of teamwork. The answer will include some discussion.

Award 5–6 marks for a detailed answer that demonstrates a sound knowledge of teamwork. The answer will contain detailed discussion.

Answers could include:
- Tasks get done more quickly.
- Tasks get done more effectively.
- Staff know what is expected of them – there are less likely to be problems.
- Staff help each other and are positive in their relationships with others.
- Happy and confident staff (staff have high self-esteem) because they know they are working well and contributing to the establishment's success.
- Better customer service so that customers want to return to the establishment.
- Staff are aware of what is happening in the rest of the establishment and want to maintain a high standard of work.
- Quality of standards is maintained.
- Good teamwork often appears effortless – but is the result of good training and management.